Your book launch has inspired us!

THE 47 YEAR OLD GIFT

ADRIAN PEARCE

With VICKI ALLEN and JAN PIERS

Adrian Mike Pearce

Jan Piers

"Love is never lost. If not reciprocated, it will flow back and soften and purify the heart."

-Washington Irving

Copyright

CONTENTS

Acknowledgements

You never write in a vacuum and this book would never have been completed without all the help from the following people.

My wife Janet, who knows a good story when she hears one and whose love and encouragement helped me push through the tough bits,

Jan Piers for her editing skills, and for having published a book herself and giving me the belief that it can be done,

Of course, Victoria (Vicki Allen) for allowing me to barge into her life and disrupt it terribly,

Don Dagenais who put us together,

Vicki and Glenn Whitely for hosting us on our visit to Vancouver Island, British Columbia,

My twin, Big Chris Pearce, for the chapter title, "When the Gift Hit the Fan,"

Thanks as well to my childhood friend, Alec Tully for his editorial help and time,

Robert Jesse Rivard for "Heartbroken Bloke a Canadian Folk Song Tale" and Janet's twin, Susan Hall, for her editing and additions to this wonderful poem.

Gord Sheppard for sending me on the path of my writing life,

Danielle Metcalfe-Chenail for her professional advice,

Shannon Tyler, of Up!99.3 for starting the buzz on the gift,

Tanara McLean for furthering the story locally,

Rob Drinkwater for taking the story to a national audience,

Roberta Bell whose CBC web story sent "The 47-Year-Old-Gift" around the world,

The Christmas Bureau of Edmonton, Darlene Kowalchuk, Executive Director, Lee Macbean, Events

and Volunteer Coordinator, and Raylene Kajner, Special Events Coordinator for the opportunity to be involved with their worthwhile organization, Gracie Jane Generoux, a well-named lady who has graciously and generously offered her venue for the opening of the 47-Year-Old-Present, as well as hosting the evening of festivities in St Albert at A Boutique Gallery Bar by Gracie Jane.
And to my dear friends, The World Famous Peckerheads, Jack Little and Vern Rutherford, and their entourage, for performing at the gift opening and for their continued support and encouragement. To anyone out there that I have missed, please forgive me if I have forgotten to mention your contribution.
I truly appreciate everyone's efforts in making this book possible.

Happy Reading!

Adrian 'Mike' Pearce

.

HEARTBROKEN BLOKE

A Canadian Folk Song Tale

by Robert Jesse Rivard and Sam Hall

REFRAIN:
It's been a hard life, a hard life to live.
For the heartbroken bloke.
For the heartbroken bloke.

The story goes a bit like this,
Witness me, short fella in the high school senior class!
It's been a hard life, a hard life to live.
For The heartbroken Bloke.
For The heartbroken Bloke.

Got a girl finally, whoopee!
Also studying, working and photographing!
It's been a hard life, a hard life to live.
For the heartbroken Bloke.
For the heartbroken Bloke.

Family now in city in a seventeenth storey apartment!
Pining for the protection the small hamlet brought!
It's been a hard life, a hard life to live.
For the heartbroken Bloke.
For the heartbroken Bloke.

Love, Love, came along, that new feeling please last forever song,
Swirling in the darkroom's light, so happy carefree me. Me!!
It's been a hard life, a hard life to live.

For the heartbroken Bloke.
For the heartbroken Bloke.

Then Monday comes, sweet heart gone, what the
hell went wrong?
She broke up with me! Just like that! I ranted and
pondered for hours,
Discovering it could be a hard life, a hard life to live.
For the heartbroken Bloke.
For the heartbroken Bloke.

Arriving home, I fired the gift under the tree!
Morning comes, baby gone, still wondering what the
hell went wrong?
Vowed never to open that gift, to forget the girl! Ah
man, and the pain!
Yes, it became a hard life, a hard life to live,
For this heartbroken bloke.
For the heartbroken bloke.

This the gift of first love sits unopened.
In the dark, under the floor, behind the basement
door.
Memory of the ecstasy of teenage love forevermore.
It's been a hard life, a hard life to live.
For the heartbroken Bloke.
For the heartbroken Bloke.

That gift of love sweet and tender, unopened for
almost 50 years long!
Yellow tape covers the dilapidated blue box of
mystery!
He crackles the wrapper, oh so, like an old love
song.
Let's open in now! Yes now... heart thumping wildly
along.

It's been a hard life, a hard life to live.
For The heartbroken Bloke.
For The heartbroken Bloke.

Wait! Always, second thoughts? Pacing back, forth!
Back it goes, ever so gently, returned to the dark, in
its spot, in the box,
Hidden again, far away, teenage love lost in time,
Still unknowing, really unfeeling, simply a small
mystery. Unopened forever more?
Wait until next year. Maybe open it on the 50th year.
It's been a hard life, a hard life to live.
For The heartbroken Bloke.
For The heartbroken Bloke.

It's been a hard life to live.

Heartbroken Bloke.
Heartbroken Bloke.
Heartbroken Bloke.

1 Lunchtime!

Our high school camera club was very elite: so elite, there were only three members, Don (Douche Bag) Dagenais, Steve (Tool Bag) Taylor and myself, Mike (Snake) Pearce.

The excitement started early in the first semester when three girls, just a year or two younger than we were, came to the door asking to join the camera club. After introducing ourselves, we asked what their level of interest or experience was. Christine, who seemed to be the leader, blurted out they thought that joining the club might be a good way to meet boys. 'Nerdy boys' she explained, as they were 'nerdy girls.' I wondered about Christine and Vicki, since both were dressed alike. Their straight brown hair, parted in the middle, cascaded down to their shoulders. Both wore dark peasant dresses printed in tiny flowers. Even their oval-framed glasses matched. The third girl was named Terri.

My friends Don and Steve were less shy around girls than I was and they decided who was going after whom. Douche Bag chose Christine and Tool

Bag chose Terri. My girl, Vicki, was the skinny, bespectacled, nerdy girl of fifteen, just two years younger than myself. Her glasses gave her a hippy look that I liked. I thought I could discern some sort of English accent. I liked that too. She had a way of expressing herself that I found amusing. Judging from the books under her arm, it looked like she was a reader. Another plus.

This all happened quickly, and however it happened, there must have been some sort of nonverbal communication taking place that was above my head, since everyone seemed pleased with the pairings. Mind you, the hard work of courting each girl still had to be accomplished.

Being in the affluent Toronto suburb of Don Mills, we enjoyed an extremely well-appointed darkroom. It had a double door entry system containing a small vestibule. The room itself had countertops and cabinets that extended to its full thirty-foot length. Goofing off one day, I climbed into one of the cabinets, closed the door and waited until Douche Bag came in to use the darkroom. In just a few minutes, he was totally focused, (pardon the pun,) on creating a print and that is when I slid open the cabinet door, screaming at him.

"You dildo head!" he yelled, volumes of spit spraying out from his braces. So much so that I worried the spit would dilute the developer and ruin his print. I laughed and laughed and laughed.

The enlarger sat in the middle of the countertop with three chemical trays to its right: one for developer, one for the stop bath, which would halt any further development, and one for the fixer, which would chemically 'fix' the print so it would not fade.

Sitting on the counter next to the enlarger was a safelight about the size of a bread box. You could slide different filters onto the front of the safelight depending on whether you were printing photos or developing film. We mostly printed photos and used a yellow filter. It cast enough of a glow to allow easy movement in the darkroom.

After a few weeks of struggling, err, I should say building trust, we managed to convince the girls to have their lunch with us in the school's darkroom, up on the second floor.

There, we had everything we needed. A portable radio, a girl each and a room with a locking outside door. Like most darkrooms, there were actually two doors. The process was to open the outside door first, close it, lock it, and only then open the second inner door.

There was a teacher with a class across the hall from us so we needed to be quiet. That was hard to do given out horny natures and three giggly girls. We came up with a foolproof system. I had already discovered that a person could hide in one of the empty cabinets under the darkroom counter; there were enough cabinets for five of us.

At the sound of a key in the lock, five of us would quietly scramble into the bottom cabinets while one of us would act as the decoy, standing at the developing trays next to the enlarger. We had even thought to keep the sliding cabinet doors open for quick access.

While we hid, the decoy would quickly turn off the radio and stuff it into the large safelight, then slide the frosted yellow filter closed, hiding it from view. Then he would gently rock an already developed picture in the first tray. That tray simply contained water. In the dark, someone unfamiliar with photo printing would not even know that the tray wasn't full of developer.

It did happen one day that the teacher from across the hall came to investigate the noises emanating from the darkroom that were disturbing her class. After unlocking the outer door, she immediately began to open the inner door. Steve, the decoy, shouted to her, "close the outside door first!" It was unusual for a student to shout at a teacher, but for the ruse to work, it was necessary. Then she had the temerity to reach for the room's light switch once through the second door. "Don't turn on the lights! You'll ruin my photograph!" said Steve.

Steve's eyes were adjusted to the dim lighting and he could see the astonished look on her face when she was confronted with a solitary figure, rocking a developer tray back and forth.

"I could have sworn I heard music and laughter coming from this room!"

"Yeah. I know. I sometimes hear it when I'm here working at lunchtime. I think it's coming through the ductwork from the lunchroom. You know how the principal allows music there now."

Hiding in the cabinets, it took everything we had not to chortle or snicker as Steve bamboozled the teacher. We had the sense to wait a beat or two after she left, until we could hear her teaching her class again, before any of us ventured out from the cabinets. Then the radio would be extracted from the safelight and the party would continue.

We were young and brash and we thought we had everyone fooled. Every club in the school had a teacher sponsor and ours was a nice guy named Harvey Goodman. Years, later, while looking through a high school yearbook, I noticed an inscription from

Mr. Goodman: "*The darkroom is for developing prints. Not romances.*"

2 Young Love

It is a warm Friday evening in the spring of 1970. Vicki and I had been dating since she and her friends had joined the camera club, eight months earlier.

Don and Christine, Vicki and I are on a double-date in downtown Toronto. Taking the TTC (Toronto Transit) to get downtown after classes was a simple matter of walking past the mansion near the school and down to Don Mills Road. One bus would take us to Pape Station on the Bloor line then we would go west five stops to Yonge Street.

On this warm spring evening with its promise of banishing winter for good, we felt all-powerful, full of the innocence of youth, totally free, with none of our future trials on any horizon. My brother Chris and I had left our part-time jobs bagging groceries and were now making much better money babysitting for many of the couples in the apartment complexes surrounding our apartment building. I had money to splurge on this date.

A guy named Peter Marshall had met us while delivering Mom's clean nursing outfits and he thought we were the answer to his problem. With so many apartment buildings in the area, he had too many customers to deliver their dry-cleaning to by himself. He offered to pay us very well; we both left the grocery store. An added bonus was that we met all these couples who wanted to hire male babysitters and were willing to pay a premium for them. We were in the money now.

It wasn't all a bed of roses. Just the other night I had gotten a severe scolding on a babysitting job. The couple, whose child I was watching, had two rules: one, no using the phone while there and two, when playing a game with their son, I was to let him win. I thought that rule was kind of warped but I let the kid win if that meant he would go to bed without any trouble.

After months of babysitting at their apartment one night a week, sometimes even two nights, I had noted that the phone never rang and I thought, what the heck. I'll call Vicki. We chatted for almost two hours about the aimless things teenagers talk about on the phone. Back then, there was no call waiting so I had no idea that the husband had tried to call several times to check up on their son and let me know they would be home later than expected.

As I heard their key in the door, I quickly signed off but not before they saw me placing the receiver into the phone's cradle. They were mad that I had disobeyed one of their rules and even angrier that they had to cut short their night out, thinking there was a problem at home and that was why the phone was in use.

I wasn't prepared to lie to them that somehow while playing with their son, the phone had come off the hook and that was why they got a busy signal. I apologized profusely and they softened their anger.

They knew I was a good babysitter and their son liked me (because I let him win?) They paid me the eight dollars for the four hours of babysitting and booked me for the next week.

On this spring evening, I had my arm around my girl, money in my pocket and two other friends to hang out with. Yonge Street was the place to be in the late sixties and early seventies. That is where everyone went. Just like here in Edmonton, we have Whyte Avenue; every city has it's 'happening' area. Toronto's just happens to be bigger.

Being hungry, we wanted to go to the "Steak and Burger" where we could get a cheap meal and maybe we could fool them into thinking we were old enough to order a beer. "Steak and Burger" was a chain that we called "Reg Rub and Keats" and there was one that Don and I frequented in the huge mall near my apartment building. At that particular one, we knew they would serve us beer. In fact, they were so helpful there that they recommended we order Labatt's Crystal. Our waiter had told us it was the coldest beer in the house. Later we learnt no one ever ordered it and the stubbies sat in the back of the fridge, always, staying nice and cold. We hoped this "Reg Rub and Keats" would be just as accommodating. They weren't. The obvious young ages of our dates put a kibosh on that idea. We did have excellent but cheap burgers though.

We rushed into the army surplus store nearby where, because of its huge inventory, it was hard for the counter staff to keep an eye on us. Donning gas masks, we careened around the back of the store pretending we were characters from the hit movie "Willard," that Vicki and Christine had just seen. I didn't know the film and assumed gas masks were part of it. I didn't care, we were having a great time.

On our way down to Union Station, we stopped in our tracks in front of an antique store. It was getting late but the place was still open. What had caught our attention was a metal figure in the window. Cast as a half devil and half animal figure, it crouched low to the ground, as though about to spring into action, its long tail curved onto its back. It emanated pure evil. And we wanted it.

This figurine was right up Vicki and Christine's alley. They delved into the supernatural, (as teens often do,) asking questions of a Ouija board or trying to read the future with Tarot cards. Once the store owner put it in our hands, we knew we had to buy it. As Christine and Don studied it appreciatively, Vicki and I pulled out our dollar bills and change onto the counter and found we had enough to pay for it and still have money left over for transit fare and whatever else might come up that evening.

The store owner was closing up so we hustled outside, feeling different somehow having that devil figure in our possession.

It was getting late and our dates had to be home at a reasonable hour, later than usual since this was not a school night. Passing a photo-booth, Vicki and I impulsively seat ourselves inside. Five shots for one dollar. Black and white. Vicki seems pensive and just as the flash goes off, I kiss her cheek as a way to console her. Buying the devil figure brings both of us down from the high of having so much fun with our friends that evening.

Two weeks later, Vicki asks me to take the figurine to my apartment. Her parents have discovered it and do not want it in their home and since we have joint custody, it's my turn to keep it.

My mother happens to be at the apartment door as I come in with the figure in my hands. I try to hide it but she has had a clear view of it. I give her some bullshit answer and rush to my room. My turn at custody lasts just a few days.

"I want that thing out of my house. Now!" My mother yells at me. In her rubber gloved hands are large pieces of broken glass, what up until a few minutes ago had been a shelf in the refrigerator that she had been cleaning.

When I brought the figurine home, I hadn't expected my mother's strong reaction. And yet, I should have known better. She had always been superstitious and had scared us as young children when telling us stories of the poltergeist that inhabited her family home in Wales, and how it would throw furniture around and break things.

Now it was decision time. What to do with the figure? Her parents and now my mother did not want it near them. I call Vicki to get her ideas on the problem. We scratch around for some time until she suggests giving it to one of her teachers that she has a good rapport with. Mr. Bleacher.

He not only accepts the figure, he also identifies it as Krampus, St. Nick's counterpart in central Europe. After handing it over, I forget all about it, for thirty-seven years anyways.

At that time, I have a phone conversation with my old friend Don (Douchebag) whom I'd found on LinkedIn. After catching up with each other's' lives, he asks me if I have heard what happened to Mr. Bleacher?

"Bleacher the Teacher?" I ask.

"That's the one. Christine and Vicki had him for some subject. He took a class on an international field trip to the Caribbean and he died while on that trip!"

My first thought was, did the devil figure have anything to do with it?

3 The End of Childhood

It was bittersweet, the summer of my fourteenth birthday. The sweetness came from our family driving to Montreal, pulling a tent trailer, to visit Expo 67. Wandering around Expo by myself allowed me to spend most of my time at the Ontario Pavilion, where I fell in love with a band called the Big Town Boys from Toronto. Sweeter still because I found a band I liked and they were located in the "Big Town" where we were to move that summer; bitter, because we would be leaving the security of our hometown. In fact, we stopped in Toronto on our way to Montreal to view the apartment we were moving into. It seemed so tiny; how was our family of six going to manage living in it after our two-storey house on a large lot in Mooretown?

In our little village, we knew everyone and had gone to school with the same class every year, from grades one through eight. We were secure in the predictability of this rural community where we had grown up. Now we were going to be hicks in the big city.

We had to spend our first summer there studying in school instead of making friends and exploring our new home. We were trying to catch up to our classmates who had been studying subjects more advanced than what we had learned at Moore Public School Number 2. We hated every moment of summer school.

The new place, an apartment, was situated on the busy corner of Don Mills Road and Sheppard Avenue. One novel feature was that the apartment was six stories high. We had never had such a lofty view. The highest we had ever been was looking out from our upstairs bedroom, over quiet, tree-lined Emily Street in Mooretown. Back there, the street was just a tar road off the main street of our little town. Not the paved, behemoth, six-lane thoroughfares in front of the apartment building.

My twin Chris and I were unhappy teenagers. We just wanted so much to fit in. Not be "hicks from the sticks." The two of us begged our father to at least let us grow our hair long enough to touch our ears. Hardly today what would be considered long hair. He would have none of it. He thought all long-haired boys were trouble.

At the supper table one night, Dad mentioned that he had met a young man with long hair in the subway. And, he added, this fellow was polite too! Chris and I jumped on this information. Was this an opportunity to crack Dad's defenses? "See Dad? We could have long hair and still be polite!" He wasn't buying it. The wedge between us was growing wider.

Months later one evening I came home to find all the lights in the apartment turned off and Mom sitting in the dark, knitting. "Why are all the lights off? And why are you sitting in the dark?" I asked.

"Your father is in the kitchen developing some film."

"Dad's in the kitchen?" This I had to see. In all my fourteen years, I could only remember my old man entering the kitchen to get another cup of coffee.

In the darkness, I could just barely make out my father's figure. He was carefully threading a roll of film onto a plastic reel made to fit into a developing tank about the size of a can of tobacco.

"Your cousin taught me about photography when your mother and I were in England," he tells me as I watch. There had been some discussion between my parents about Dad needing a hobby to take his mind off his stressful work. Before we had even moved to Toronto, Dad's doctor had prescribed nitroglycerin for his angina. He kept the pills in a small ampule hanging off a thin chain around his neck. I thought my father looked odd wearing a necklace and often caught myself thinking about it.

I was quite fascinated with the photographic process. My father, an engineer, was only too happy to explain in great detail the full procedure. Spending time like this with Dad was a novel experience since we had grown so far apart, partly because, well, I was a teenager and I was angry and unhappy with his decision to move us to this huge city.

Over many months, we began to spend more time together in the kitchen, measuring chemicals, mixing them with water at just the right temperature (sixty-eight degrees.) My interest in the whole thing grew to such a point that I eventually took over the kitchen as often as I could. Dad went back to sitting in his easy chair and reading the day's paper after supper.

One evening, I heard Mom, as she looked up from her knitting, say, "you know Don, that hobby was supposed to be for you. To help you relax."

"Kit, (my father's pet name for Mom) it is relaxing enough to know exactly where one of my teenage sons is every evening!"

My first year of high school was about to begin and I was filled with anxiety. My twin brother would be going to a different school than I for the first time. We wouldn't have each other's support. I didn't have any cool clothes to wear and thanks to Dad, I had a square haircut. How was I going to cope? Chris and I had made a few neighbourhood friends over the past few summers. The wrong sort of friends. Happily, none of them would be going to my new school. That meant that the only person I would know there was my sister Hilary. She was going into her most senior year while I was entering my most junior year.

Someone at the Board of Education must have mixed up our two files. My brother, who had the better marks would be going to Georges Vanier, a trade school, while I, with my poor marks, would be enrolled at George S. Henry, an academic institution. At least it was a smaller school whereas Chris' was a huge education factory.

Walking to school meant crossing over the 401. I remember it was seventeen lanes wide at that point in time. My route involved a steep incline past an old mansion to the school grounds. On that first day, it seemed forever long, forlorn and almost insurmountable.

My one ray of hope that day was that, amazingly, I recognized a friend I had made in junior high. Nial Hamilton. Everyone mispronounced his name as Ny-al instead of Neil. Both he and I liked the same music and would spend our time hanging out with his older brother, who played in the very same band I loved at Expo 67, The Big Town Boys!

Slowly, I adjusted to my new surroundings and began to appreciate Toronto and its eclectic corners. With my new interest in photography, I explored areas like Cabbagetown, and Yonge Street and stores like Sam the Record Man and Honest Ed's. I was young, ready for adventure and the big city was seducing me.

4 Loss of Innocence

At sixteen, my childhood ended. I began to take on the responsibilities of a man. It was just Mom and Chris and I living in the apartment now. Dad had died from a massive heart attack and our two older sisters, Jay and Hilary, had already left home to enter nursing school.

The elevators in the new seventeen-storey apartment building we had moved into were not working. Mom and Dad had been out grocery shopping and had to trudge up the stairs. After watching the Cosby Show, we had all gone to bed. Chris and I were awoken to the sounds of our mother screaming. There was Dad sprawled across the bathroom floor, smelling like Avon's Skin So Soft bath oil. I didn't know what to do so I ran down the stairs to the lobby. Chris had already called 911 while Mom cradled Dad's head in her lap. My idea was to direct the firemen and paramedics to the seventeenth floor. All in vain. Dad died on his way to the hospital.

Our mother was at a total loss. Dad had done everything: paid the rent, balanced the checkbook, was the sole family provider. What were we going to do? Mom had been a nurse during the war. Her training was obsolete. But at the age of fifty-seven, she went back to school and graduated as a nurse's aide and began working at North York General Hospital. She had secured work in the hardest unit, hardest physically and emotionally, in the burn unit.

My brother and I helped out financially with part time jobs after school and in the summer. We were each hurting in our own way. We pulled away from each other, internalizing our individual anguish. We were each in our own personal hell.

Yet life continued. High school classes needed attending. In a math class, someone behind me was laughing. I turned around and told him to shut up. In my grief, I couldn't believe that at a time like this that there could be laughter in the world. I got up and left the classroom, never to take that subject again.

Our local Dominion store manager hired my twin brother and I to bag groceries after school. Slowly, painfully, each of us at our own pace passed through our grief in its many stages, rejoined the living and adjusted to our new reality.

5 The Break Up

Smoking a pipe, I felt gave me an air of sophistication to match my status as a high school guy with a girlfriend. I had grown up with my father smoking a pipe, so it wasn't a far stretch for me to take it up. While Dad favoured straight-stemmed pipes, my choice was one with a slight downward bend that I thought wouldn't put as much pressure on my crooked teeth. The pipe also took a filter, which, according to the ads in Popular Mechanics, made smoking this pipe a healthy and pleasurable experience.

Across from the school, a thick layer of wet Toronto snow covered the grass in the park where all the smokers hung out. My habit was to meet Vicki there before class but today my penny loafers were getting soaked in the slush on the ground from so many feet mashing the once white snow. With only minutes to go before the buzzer rang, I could see her coming toward the park. There was something different about her today. I couldn't quite put my finger on it but I was sure I would find out while enjoying a smoke with her.

We used to joke that she smoked a brand that anyone would know was Canadian from its name: Export eh? She hadn't said much by the time I lit her cigarette with my fancy pipe lighter. Its pressurized fuel cylinders produced a long jet of flame that could light pipe tobacco buried deep inside a pipe bowl.

"I have something to tell you," she starts off. I knew she wasn't pregnant since we had yet to have sex. Was she quitting school? Moving? Whatever it was, it must be serious from the expression on her face.

"I'm breaking up with you. I've met someone else and I can't date two guys at the same time."

"What??? You can't be serious! Who is this other guy? Have you been cheating? I'll go punch him out!" This couldn't be happening. What a Christmas surprise! Yet I shouldn't have been too shocked since I had the feeling yesterday that she was avoiding my repeated phone calls. Her sister Stephanie said that Vicki was out Christmas shopping and she didn't know when she'd be home.

Stephanie, Vicki's younger sister was a good egg in my estimation. I liked her because she was happy to accept one of my quarters and then take her time going to the variety store for candy. A cheap ploy I used so I could be alone with her sister. The two of them shared a bedroom so it was absolutely necessary to get Steph out of the way. I'm sure she suspected we were up to no good, but so far, she hadn't ratted us out to her parents.

I reeled from the news. I really had thought that Vicki and I had something going and to find this out just before Christmas was mean. My family and I were bracing for another Christmas without Dad.

Last Christmas, the first one without him, was horrible and this one now looked like it was shaping up to be just as miserable. Now my girlfriend was dumping me.

From her purse she hands me a small gift wrapped in blue foil paper, complete with a gift tag taped under some holiday ribbon. "What is this?" I ask.

"It's a little something I bought for you when I was Christmas shopping. When I met this boy. His name is John Wolf but he likes to be called Wolfie."

"Oh, so this just happened? This 'Wolfie' guy? Just get rid of him. I'll forgive you," I was desperate. With the prospect of losing my girlfriend on top of a shitty Christmas, I was willing to bargain. No dice. She wouldn't even consider it.

I didn't want her to see my tears so I turned away from her. I heard the school buzzer go off as I stomped through the snow with one thought, that I needed to be home to lock myself in my room and never come out again. To hell with classes and to hell with Vicki. It was a long trudge down to Don Mills Road, the tiny present still in my hand.

No one was home when I threw the present under the tree. A few gifts had already collected there. Mom must have put them under the tree early to try to lend some cheer to our still sad household. My brother and I were still taking sleeping pills every night before bed to ensure we slept through the night. We were both resisting falling asleep since we were afraid of being woken in the middle of the night to our mother's screams.

After the holiday, Mom was taking down the decorations from the tree. She pointed out that I still had that unopened gift under it.

"I'm never opening that gift," I said with as much vehemence as I could muster. A few days later, I found it in my room. My mother must have moved it there when the Christmas tree disappeared. I threw it into a seldom used drawer and slammed it shut.

It was painful to see Vicki in the hallways at school. I couldn't help but to run into her as the school had only six hundred students. I was still hurting from being dumped. My male pride was bruised. To assuage my ego, I developed a story that this 'Wolfie' guy was older and a member of a motorcycle gang. With the creation of this fiction, I could rationalize what had happened to me. My friends would say, "I wouldn't have stood a chance either. Not with an older guy with a motorcycle."

I could see how she had changed; wilder, somehow more sophisticated, more grown up. She was dressing differently. She and Christine weren't dressing alike anymore. And she looked sexier, which didn't help matters at all. She and Christine would be laughing as they skipped down the hallways. This Wolfie was a bad influence on her. He was leading her down the garden path. Johnny Winter's song "Be Careful with A Fool" ran through my mind. Yep. That's me. A fool.

This was my last year of high school. I was in grade thirteen and that brought some flexibility in my schedule. We could pick and choose which subjects we wanted to study. With Dad gone, I could drop math and the sciences and still have enough credits to graduate. Our mother was too busy doing her own studying to pay much attention to what my brother and I were doing.

I dropped the camera club as I was working five days a week after school at Imperial Oil's head office in Don Mills. The job gave me a lot of satisfaction; serving cafeteria food to the company's late workers. One bus ride would get me there early enough to help out in the preparation of the food I would be serving that evening and I was learning something about cooking. Still smarting from the breakup, I was developing a crush on Lynda, a recently graduated apprentice chef who worked in the kitchen. She encouraged my interest in cooking but discouraged my interest in her.

There was still one girl I could ask out, Ronnie Blackburn, the daughter of one of my father's friends. My brother and I had lusted after her since our first meeting at a family dinner at their home in an upscale Toronto neighbourhood. She was our age and much more cosmopolitan than we two hicks.

When I say I could ask her out, in my mind I was dating her. In her mind, here was a guy she could hang out with. My brother assured me that she only went out with me because she knew I would never try anything. I was too timid. Yet I was okay enough to be with. I knew she was a popular girl and had her choice of jocks to go out with so I was always pleased when she agreed to do things with me.

One of my favourite bands, Canned Heat, was playing at Varsity Arena and I wanted to go but not alone. Ronnie agreed to join me. The band wasn't the same as the one I had grown to love. Their co-founder, Alan "Blind Owl" Wilson had died the year before from a drug overdose yet the band was still riding the charts and had recently come out with a new album, "Historical Figures and Ancient Heads," which I had just bought at Sam the Record Man on Yonge Street.

The great thing about being with Ronnie Blackburn was that she was cool. Everyone wanted to be near her. This concert was no different. Those around us wanted to turn her on. Joint after joint was handed to her. When she passed them to me, I declined.

Two hours of listening to the backup bands, Rod Stewart, and the Faces and the Motor City 5 only heightened my desire to see and hear Canned Heat.

While the roadies set up the band's gear, I looked around the venue. Varsity Arena had a curved ceiling much like a Quonset hut. Suddenly, I imagined that I was in the St. George subway station; the same one we had exited to come to the concert. I kept shaking my head and looking around to reassure myself of my surroundings. I could not believe how heightened my imagination had become. Was this effect just from being near Ronnie?

Spending that afternoon with Ronnie helped me get over Vicki. I went home with a smile on my face, thinking there is a girl out there who wants to do things with me.

6 How Michael Dodged a Bullet, by Vicki Allen

During the first two years of high school as an honours student, the biggest question on my mind was, "just what the hell kind of meat is in the meat pies that we eat every day?" Fatty, full of gristle, edible only when smothered in ketchup, the meat pies were the single cafeteria item at George S. Henry Secondary School that my friends and I were willing to scarf down.

But by the third year of high school, everything changed. Suddenly, the grades seemed unimportant, we acknowledged that the menu wasn't about to improve and the big mystery became, "what does a girl have to do to be one of the popular people, one of the 'in' crowd?"

Completely incapable of figuring it out on my own, I handed over my pretty much non-existent social life to my best high school friend, who logically and methodically came up with a plan that I was just wish-washy enough to go along with, awed by her genius.

There were three of us, three fifteen-year-old females who were pretty sure that getting on the popularity radar was, in eleventh grade, our entire reason for going to school each day. As the plan emerged, it seemed to be foolproof. Identify an extracurricular activity predominantly attended by males, fake enthusiasm for the subject and join the club, then discreetly pursue the obvious.

Of course, it wasn't that cut-and-dried, but hindsight nearly fifty years later tells me that a lot of the best advice I have given as an adult to divorced friends has been based on the simplified strategy of those high school machinations. I might wish the advice was original to me, but credit where it's due. If you want to pursue someone, go where they are likely to be; no point in waiting for them to find you.

The Camera Club was the perfect fit for our purposes. At the beginning of the term, its membership was solely male and all three of us young women could figure out which end of the camera to look through. Black and white film was inexpensive, and the intricacies of developing and processing were a perfect excuse to require help as we crowded into the small area allotted to the club's activities or around the photographic enlarger.

Sweet heaven, but this sounds terribly duplicitous. Does it help that we were completely unaware that we were teenagers who had yet to discover that the 'free love of the '70's' was our demographic?

So, there we were. Unremarkable except for that plan. And it worked in some respects. The three of us found something in common with the three unattached senior males who, fortunately for us, were not embarrassed to be 'paired up' with juniors.

Having a boyfriend in high school elevated us to a status we'd only dreamed of. After being nearly invisible for two years, even the teachers knew who we were, although not always for the right reasons, because school, both attendance and grades, took a backseat to our social lives. Suddenly we were dedicated to the pursuit of the perfect nail polish colour, not the precision of conjugating Latin verbs or painstakingly dissecting frogs in biology.

It was lovely. The three of us spent endless hours discussing possibilities, boasting of mostly unmet romantic milestones and avoiding responsibilities, instead of swatting textbooks and watching endless hours of horror movies, which had pretty much been our obsession before we set out to define ourselves by boys in our lives.

In hindsight, I am annoyed with myself and the prevalent for the times teenage insecurities that prompted the plan. Young women don't need males to define them, let alone validate their existence. But in the early '70's, we were somewhat trapped in an unexamined transition period between the ideal domestic goddess, June Cleaver, and the eventual emergence of the Divine Miss M, closely followed by the newly awakened revelations of Janet Weiss in The Rocky Horror Picture Show.

When I think about the pairings that occurred in high school, I realize that many of the girls had enough common sense to seek out guys who were destined, even then, to make something, someone of themselves, recognizing ambition for success and carefully positioning themselves to be factored into that potential being realized. I can admire, however, that many of my classmates selected excellent candidates with whom to build a future, then made themselves indispensable to that future. That requires a level of common sense and level-headedness I somehow did not acquire, then or later.

And so, the pairing of myself with Mike, as I shall forever think of him, was doomed, despite the strong likelihood that he was the perfect candidate for a good run of forty, fifty or more years. Perhaps it was due to my naivety at the time; I think more likely, it was because I had yet to fully embrace the rebellious nature that was probably at the root of why I hadn't 'fit in' in high school in the first place. I did eventually come to terms with that, though; learning that my desire, my inclination, my preference to be unconventional suited me fine despite the fact that it continuously horrified my parents, among others.

My denouement of our exercise in popularity came about almost entirely thanks to that very same genius who created the plan in the first place. We were at Yorkdale Mall, having shopped for Mike's Christmas gift, when my cohort-in-crime spotted some badass dude walking around with mistletoe clipped to his pocket. With all the confidence in the world, most recently from finding her place as a popular high school student at last, she asked him what it was for.

He held it over MY head, bent me backwards over his arm, right there in the mall, and he kissed me. It was romantic. It was the stuff of Harlequins (another obsession of ours prior to that year.) It begged to be a Kodak moment.

But there you go. He kissed me in front of the mall gods and a huge crowd of Christmas shoppers, including people, such as my girlfriend, who were likely to report it back to Mike. I had crossed a line.

Because I returned the kiss.

Merry Christmas Mike.

7 What's Cooking?

Hot vomit spewed out of my mouth onto my place setting at the head table inside Canada Packers banquet room. Our cooking class had been touring the packing plant all morning and now we were being treated to a roast beef lunch. I was seated at the head table simply because I was dating the only girl in our class, Collette. She was very cute and in our male dominated cooking class of 1973, every guy wanted her attention.

It was the sight of the thick, blubbery translucent fat on the outside of the roast jiggling as the chef sawed slices of prime rib that did me in. All morning we had been subjected to horrible sights, sounds and smells. We'd even had to take cover as a deranged steer had gotten loose and was charging about the second floor of the plant. I was sure the huge animal was going to slip on the slick floor and crash through the glass brick walls plunging onto the traffic congested St. Clair Avenue below.

During my last year at George S. Henry, I had been working at Imperial Oil's head office every day after school. The job didn't involve cooking as much as serving up dinner and drinks in the cafeteria and taking the customer's money. After eight o'clock, I was responsible for putting all the food away and then cashing out. It was simple and I enjoyed working on my own. An apprentice chef named Lynda was working there and encouraged my interest in cooking. She was older than me and experienced enough to see that I had a crush on her, which she quickly discouraged. She was already taken. When Lynda discovered my interest in cooking (I had been experimenting at home with my mother's help), she convinced me to enroll at George Brown College.

How I managed to snag the only girl in our class is still beyond me. I hadn't dated anyone since my breakup with Vicki and I was shy around girls. Much later, Collette told me that she became interested in me when she saw me take off my shirt in class one day. I didn't realize I had that much of a physique. Something about my shoulders caught her attention. Go figure!

That is how I ended up being at the head table at Canada Packers; ralphing on the table in front of my classmates and instructors was bad enough however it was still early days with Collette and I wanted to impress her. It was lucky for me that the manager of the packing plant was quite smitten with her and holding her attention. She hardly noticed my plight.

George Brown College where our cooking classes were held was right in the heart of Kensington Market, a place made famous a few years later by the CBC television show "King of Kensington," a situation comedy that was a huge Canadian success.

Just blocks away from our campus was the El Mocambo Tavern, made famous six years later when the Rolling Stones played there and recorded a live album. It was rumoured at that time that Margaret Trudeau was having a fling with Mick Jagger at that famous establishment.

Collette and I became a thing late in the first semester of cooking school. A few of us had gathered in our friend Rico's basement to party and celebrate the Christmas break. Collette happened to be sitting on the floor beside the couch where I was sprawled out. We were all listening to Rico's newest album, "Woodstock." Alvin Lee's fingers were tearing up and down the fretboard blasting out "I'm Goin' Home."

I reached down and touched her shoulder. It's like my arm became an electrical conduit connecting the two of us. She must have been waiting for me to make a move since, in moments, she was on the couch and in my arms. All those hours in class dreamily staring at her and now I am kissing her.

Our friends didn't seem to mind our passionate display and maybe, just maybe they had been watching us over the past weeks and seen something brewing between us that I was too naive to see. There wasn't enough time to tell her how I felt as she was leaving for home right after the party. I was ecstatic! That warm loving feeling I had missed for so long filled me and I knew I was going to have a great Christmas this year.

As soon as I got home to the apartment I shared with my brother and my mother, I began to send Collette telegrams professing my love for her. Yes! I was in love! I now had my first girlfriend since Vicki had dumped me.

After the Christmas break and our joyful reunion, I appreciated how the guys in our class respected us dating. They knew she was off limits while she was dating me. Mind you, that didn't stop our ex-con classmate from making passes at her. He knew damn well I wasn't going to do anything about it.

One night, a group of us went to see Fats Domino at the El Mocambo. I'm glad I insisted we arrive early for the show as that resulted in us having front row seats, just a few feet from the stage. During the rousing show, the sax players were close enough that in our excitement, we threw money into the horns of their instruments. We were having a riot and when Fats began to push the piano across the stage with his huge belly, the crowd went wild.

This was one of the best times I'd had in a long while. The El Mocambo was where the likes of Muddy Waters and Buddy Guy had performed and you could feel the history of the place wrap around you like a warm comforter. Here I'm with a gorgeous girl, surrounded by my friends and seeing one of my favourite artists in a very cool place. Life was suddenly good.

This young woman was pretty, funny and sharp as a tack. She was a great cook too. And just as importantly, my mother liked her. My mother had never really approved of Vicki and it was mostly my fault for missing curfew after curfew, wanting to spend as much time as I could with Vicki. Plus, she lived an hour's walk from our place so a lot of the times that I was late, I was simply walking home, saving on bus fare.

My mother and Collette would have long discussions about china. Not the country but the fine stuff used for making and drinking tea. The good dinnerware that would be brought out on special occasions. I didn't know a Delft from a Damask but the two of them could go on and on for hours it seemed. Seeing the two of them happy together made me happy.

Things got a little awkward when Collette took me home to her family farm in Southern Ontario, not far from the shores of Lake Erie. Her parents were polite to me but not very warm. I already knew about Collette's romance with her high school sweetheart and I got the strong impression that her parents wanted her to get back together with him. That way, she would live near them and, as well, his family owned a successful business which would ensure a good and stable life for her. Isn't that what we all want for our daughters?

If their welcome wasn't very encouraging, things got weirder when her father and brother were about to go work in the fields. They looked at me as though it was expected that I would join them. They gave me questioning looks when I begged off, saying I'd rather stay with Collette and help her and her mother with the cooking.

Strange looks continued throughout the lunch we had prepared and I caught Collette's parents exchanging knowing glances across the table. I was certain that when they got her alone, they would pressure her to leave me and continue with her old boyfriend.

Once we graduated from George Brown, certificates in hand, many of us went in different directions. One got a job preparing meals at the airport, another went back to his home town of Paris, (Ontario), Collette took a position at a remote hunting lodge and I chose Stratford, not far from my family in London, Ontario.

Separating from Collette left me feeling anxious, fearful for our future. The very fact that we had chosen different places for our apprenticeships, was an ominous sign to me.

A few of us from the class would be working at the Stratford Inn, preparing meals for the many tourists visiting the Stratford Festival. Growing up, Mom and Dad had taken us there many times to see Shakespearean plays (which bored us children,) and Gilbert and Sullivan operas (which thrilled us.)

Three of us decided to rent a place together in town. The only apartment we could afford was a hovel above a derelict store in the neglected downtown. Paul, my sister Jay's husband, helped me move a fridge up the long and steep staircase. We had demanded it when we discovered the apartment didn't have one. It was a deal breaker until the landlord acquiesced and provided one if we moved it into the dump. Paul and I had been friends for as long as he had known my sister Jay. He would do anything for me; even hump a fridge, weighing several hundred pounds to a place I wouldn't show anyone else: tells you what kind of place this was and what kind of friend I had in Paul.

Things weren't going very well for me at the Stratford Inn. Even though I wasn't experienced, they made me the egg chef. There is no diner fussier than one at breakfast. Plate after plate was returned to the kitchen because the eggs weren't cooked to the guest's satisfaction. The head chef was not pleased. My other classmates were working different shifts so we never saw enough of each other to compare notes, although I suspect they were making out better as they had paid more attention in class than I had. I was too distracted thinking about Collette.

The remoteness of the hunting lodge where Collette worked meant that I hadn't heard from her in six weeks. That's a long time to be away from your girlfriend. One day I received a wrinkled postcard from Algonquin Park where she was working. The front showed the lodge with its red metal roof and rugged exterior. Turning the card over, the only thing she had written in her neat printing was "Miss you!" That was it. They worked her so hard that she had no more time to write anything else? Was a bear chasing her or something?

When she arrived at our apartment a few weeks later during a short break, she was happy to see me and her old classmates. My happiness was short-lived when she admitted that she had been with someone else. Grief is defined as "deep sorrow, especially that caused by someone's death." Someone might not have died that day, but a relationship had. With time, having gotten to stage five; acceptance, I can respect her honesty but at the time I couldn't believe that in only a matter of weeks she had been unfaithful to me. That is stage one; denial. The next stage, anger, quickly consumed me. I left her in my room while I went for a walk. Walking is something that has always calmed me when I'm upset.

Stage three, bargaining, was mostly ignored when I got back to the apartment. She wanted to discuss the situation, but I would have none of it. I asked her as calmly as I could to just go back into the room. I would sleep on the couch and when I woke up, I hoped she'd be gone.

It would have been better if I had bargained with her. Or at least if I had tried to hear her out. What was coming right at me down the grief highway was depression. A funk that affected my work which wasn't going very well anyway and it was getting even deeper, living in that squalid apartment. Within a couple of days, I went to the head chef (with egg on my face) and quit. He almost did a little jig. He wouldn't have to fire me after all.

We have had no contact since that time although my sister Hilary, who lives in southern Ontario, has run into her when visiting a nearby town. Collette was happily working in a jewellery and china shop. Maybe she went on to live the life her parents so wanted for her.

Moving back to London, where my sister and mother lived, I managed to get a job at a Disney-themed restaurant called the Seven Dwarfs. With my short stature, I fit right in! However, being a hot-headed young male, I didn't fit in with the hyper demanding head chef. I disagreed with how the kitchen was being managed and I was disgusted enough to quit. I didn't want to be a chef anymore. My heart had gone out of it.

8 London Love

Was I ever going to have a relationship that didn't flounder in a matter of months? I started looking. Living at home with my mother was good for the two of us but I was lonely in London without a girlfriend. I had considered asking Heather Dyble for a date, she felt more like a sister to me since we had grown up together. Her mother had befriended my mother when I was still a wee lad. Our families became quite close and we often visited back and forth and spent holidays together.

The real reason that I could not ask Heather out was that I was embarrassed. I had been in the hospital where Heather was training to be a nurse. I'd had the varicose veins stripped out of my left leg, the condition was the result of the transfusions I received as a baby. The operation was supposed to happen when I turned sixteen but then Dad died and everything changed. Now I was nineteen and working at a job at the London Free Press that required me to stand on a concrete floor all day long.

It was agony. My legs, especially the left one, were killing me. So, I sought medical help.

After the operation, while I was in bed recuperating, the head nurse came by with a gaggle of student nurses (is that what they call a group of nurses?) and asked if she could show them the results of my vein stripping. Wanting to be a cooperative patient (remember, my mother and two sisters were nurses,) I assented. What I hadn't anticipated was her whipping off the whole bedsheet that was covering me and exposing my naked lower half to the nursing students. I was totally scored out having a bevy of beautiful young women observe me in such a vulnerable position. To make matters worse, Heather was one of them. That was the end of any thoughts I might have had about asking her out.

My friend Tim from Mooretown who I'd been hanging out with, had a girlfriend named Karen who had a cute, single girlfriend named Joan. They described her as a nice girl and thought we would be a good match. Why is it couples always want to match up their single friends?

With a full red beard, long reddish-brown hair and sporting large tortoise shell aviator glasses, would I be a good match for this cute girl? I was eager, so I agreed to going on a blind date. Tim and Karen had the idea of a movie at the drive-in as a brilliant way for the two of us to meet.

Joan was seated in the backseat of Tim's car when they came to pick me up. I was nervous about meeting this girl and having the drive-in as our first encounter. In my circle of friends, the only time you went to the drive-in with a girl was to make out. Is this what this was all about? Didn't they say she was a nice girl?

I hadn't met Karen yet although I had heard lots of good things about her while hanging out with Tim. I climbed into the back and introduced myself to Karen and Joan. Joan was very cute with a slight pixie nose that I liked. Her blonde hair was cut in a fashionable shag and she was well groomed. I thought she was a knock-out. Wow! Was this my date?

Joan had a cute little girl's voice and she used to answer my barrage of questions. Finding out about someone is a technique I use when meeting for the first time, especially if I am nervous and trying to establish some common ground. Her lips looked inviting and I hoped to get the chance to kiss them.

As the two of us kibitzed with Tim and Karen, this allowed us both to relax. I had concerns about what she thought of me, how I looked, etc. I didn't think she was instantly attracted to me, yet she wasn't repelled either. We were going to a drive-in after all and that meant that three of us in the car had certain expectations (Tim, Karen and I.) Joan's thoughts on the matter had yet to be discovered.

Not long after the trailers were through, I saw Tim put his arm around Karen. I looked over at Joan and put my arm around her. She leaned into me. She kinda likes me, I'm thinking. When Tim and Karen started to make out, the two of us took that as a signal to do the same. It would have been totally awkward to try to watch the film through their twisting bodies, what with the smacking of their lips and the moaning and groaning that was coming from the front seat.

We didn't get too heavy but heavy enough that I wanted to see her again. When I asked for a second date, she agreed. It was looking like I was going to have a girlfriend after all.

It's hard to say if her parents totally approved of me. Having a daughter myself, I understand now how they may have felt. Was this guy good enough for our daughter Joan? He has a job at the Free Press and he seems to want to better himself and go back to school. We're not sure about his long red beard and his long hair, but our daughter is happy.

Mom didn't share the same connection with Joan that she'd had with Collette. Collette liked to cook and was good at it. Mom had started to prepare elaborate meals using my French cooking manual from school and she and Collette spent hours together in the kitchen experimenting with new techniques.

Joan was so pretty that I constantly took photos of her and unlike Vicki, she was a willing subject. With a photo model like Joan, I could experiment with my photography at. My favourite picture of her is a black and white photo taken shortly after swimming one afternoon. In it she is wearing a collared tank top, buttons open all the way, exposing her bikini top. The photo is high contrast with strong lighting coming from over her shoulder, her body turned slightly toward the camera. Wet hair slicked back, her face is open and she smiles seductively at the camera. I had never photographed her this way and I liked this look. She looks so young and sexy but also innocent somehow. The strong blacks and whites in the photo would make my future photography instructor, Ludi Dietrich, very happy. He wouldn't be throwing this one on the ground.

Often, when I picked Joan up she wouldn't be ready. (Big surprise there, eh?) Her mother would suggest that I go downstairs and have a drink with Joan's father. A small and quiet man, I would often find him with elbows perched on the bar as though he had been there a long time, sipping a rye and ginger. He would offer me one and we would sit there awkwardly fumbling for something to talk about. My attempts at conversation were often met with stony silence. He looked defeated. Was his wife the source of his troubles? They say that when you are interested in a girl, look at the mother. You could be looking at your future wife.

The thought had crossed my mind since Joan and I were getting serious about being together. My problem right then was that I knew my job at the Free Press was coming to an end soon and I wanted to go back to school, to a school in Toronto. What was going to happen to our relationship?

After leaving the Seven Dwarfs restaurant, my brother-in-law Paul's father found me a position at the local paper. A newspaper that my brother Chris and I had delivered in Mooretown when we were ten and eleven years old. I was back in the newspaper business. The job involved operating a Linotype machine that through a complicated mechanical process, produced the type for the paper.

The job was repetitive but did require rapt attention since as an operator, you were dealing with molten lead. One day when I was especially bored, a fellow wearing a leather jacket rushed past my machine. He looked like something out of Indiana Jones, an exciting and adventurous individual. I asked my supervisor Alfie, who was that guy? He explained that the family who owned the paper also owned CFPL, the local television station. This particular guy was a news film cameraman and he was here to get his film processed before taking it back to the station for editing.

Turning back toward my machine, my mind was filled with images of being at exciting events: fires, accidents, maybe even doing some travelling. While living at home in Toronto, my brother and I were devoted fans of WKBW's Irv Weinstein whose "Action News" made Buffalo seem like an exotic, faraway place, even though it was just across Lake Ontario. On a clear day, we could make out Buffalo from our seventeenth-floor apartment. We liked the place names of the fire locations; Tonawanda, Cheektowaga, Lackawanna. Irv kept us informed every night of the seemingly endless string of fires in that city. Buffalo must be a city of arsonists, we thought.

The reverie was still playing in my mind when the cameraman whooshed past my Linotype machine yet again. Seeing him for the second time and knowing what he did for a living, I made a life altering decision. I pointed at him and said, "that's what I want to do!" My job at the London Free Press was coming to an end as it was being phased out by computer technology. I was ready to move on. I only had to figure out a way to get from being a Linotype operator to being a news film cameraman.

In the '70's without the internet, my research was done at the main branch of the London Public Library. The local college, Fanshawe had a program on television arts, as did Conestoga in Kitchener-Waterloo. I knew Ryerson in Toronto taught film but it was a degree program and I wanted something more practical. I wanted a job, not a degree. Humber too had a cinematography program and I remembered the place fondly from having photographed a rock concert there. I sent away for all these college's course guides.

Within two weeks, I had a slew of paper catalogues to thumb through. Ryerson was out, Fanshawe didn't seem serious enough, I knew nothing about Conestoga so it seemed my decision was going to be Humber College. The description of their three-year creative cinematography program suited my needs.

Since the age of fourteen when Dad had interested me in photography, I had been taking pictures and developing them. Yet I never wanted to be a professional photographer; photographing weddings, christenings and the like. I knew about exposure, composition, shutter speeds and I figured that all those principals would apply to film, the only difference being I would be taking twenty-four pictures a second rather than one at a time.

My twin Chris was living in Toronto, studying stage management, never having made the move to London with Mom and I. Our sisters had long ago left home to become nurses. My brother and I agreed to find a place to live together. Once again, Paul helped me to locate something we could afford. We ended up choosing a two bedroom in a Jewish neighbourhood that had for us, one big bonus. We could get fresh bagels anytime we liked at a local bakery.

Joan was unhappy with my decision to go to Humber College however we both agreed to stay in our relationship and make it work long distance. When I started studying at Humber, I poured myself into my studies. You see, I had always thought that I was stupid. That stemmed from all those times in the past, when my twin and I would hand over our report cards and our parents would immediately see my lousy marks. Inevitably they would ask, "why are your marks so low and your brother's marks are so high? You are twins after all. They should be the same." I would just shrug and feel dumb.

What I discovered at Humber was that I wasn't daft. The problem was that I had never been taught a subject I was interested in until then. There, I excelled. I received honours every year for the three years I was there.

There was little time for anything other than school. Little time for Joan. When we did talk, it was all about my new experiences. My new friends. The only thing that had changed for her was that she had moved out of her parent's house and into a townhouse she shared with a roommate. I began to think of Joan as the hometown girl. Pining for her guy, keeping herself for him. I could hear it in her voice when we talked on the phone. To me, she was being clingy. We were growing apart and I was the one doing most of the growing. I didn't want to be chained down to the girl back home. It wasn't like I had a romantic interest in anyone here, I was just focused on my studies.

Out of respect for her, I didn't feel I could continue this way. I knew I was becoming a new person. I guess you could say that I was defining myself. Joan was a sweet person and I was beginning to feel that I was leading her on, pretending that I was still interested in her when in fact, I only wanted to study being a cameraman. I didn't want to feel an obligation to always having to go back to London to see her.

I had to end our relationship and forty-two years later, I still feel shitty about how I did it.

Taking the train to London one Friday afternoon, I pondered how I was going to break up with her. It wasn't going to be easy. I still cared for her but I wanted my freedom. Visiting her that same evening, I was caught off guard. She had gotten a new job. She was reinventing herself. She was wearing a sexy uniform that made her look like an airline stewardess. Great hair, attractive makeup, a sleek outfit that included a scarf. I have this silk scarf thing. Never mind; I was captivated.

She felt just as happy seeing me and we hurried upstairs to her bedroom. We had a passionate night but when I awoke 'the morning after,' I came to my senses. What was I doing? My plan was to break up with her. Not rekindle our romance. I hopped out of bed waking her. "Why are you getting dressed?" she asked.

"I have to leave you. I cannot continue on like this."

"What are you saying?"

"I'm breaking up with you. I don't want to be with you anymore!"

I hurriedly left the townhouse feeling like a complete asshole. I had just slept with her and now I am breaking up? What a horrible thing to do to someone. It was not my proudest moment.

Joan would call me in Toronto. Feeling guilty, I always took her calls and we would talk. She would plead to get back together again. As much as a jerk that I had been, I had to be true to my heart. I had to focus on my studies and not be distracted by the girl back home. I had to tell her over and over that we were done.

We never dated again, but we did see one another in my second year, when she left her vehicle in our parking stall, at the apartment where I was now living with two of my classmates, Bill and Victor. None of us had cars so we had a space available for hers. I had sold her my Pontiac Parisienne when I moved back to Toronto and that is the car she left in our space. She was flying out of Pearson and didn't want to pay for parking. Maybe she thought that connecting with me would rekindle the spark we once had.

9 Seven Years Later

I was lonely in Toronto in my first year of school, although I had lots of company, that is of the insect variety. Cockroaches to be exact. I could hear the scuttling of hundreds of them every time I turned on a light. I rarely saw my twin and I wondered why he even needed an apartment. God only knew where he stayed. Maybe he was sowing his wild oats? He did pay his share of the rent which was a good thing. I was on a student loan with only so much money. Oddly enough I was considered an orphan by the Ontario student loan people, and that meant that half of my student loan was a grant that didn't have to be repaid. Still, I had only so much money. But I was on my way to being a news film cameraman.

Seven years had passed since my breakup with Vicki and the present was back home with my stuff that I stored at my mother's place.

It was Stephanie, Vicki's sister who put us back in touch. Our college had a cafeteria/hangout place called "The Pipe," named for all the exposed heating and ventilation ductwork that was painted in bright colours that hung above our heads. Steph approached while I was having lunch with my classmates. Raised eyebrows and jealous looks from my friends greeted her arrival at our table. My! What a difference seven years can make. She was gorgeous and perhaps that is why she was in the fashion program at the college. She had to introduce herself as she had changed so much, I did not recognize her. She was no longer a little kid to be brushed off with a quarter; now what stood in front of me was a very attractive young woman.

We left my smirking friends to speak privately and she tells me two things. One, that her sister Vicki would like to see me, (how did she know I was there?) and if I saw Vicki, to ask about her nose. (Her nose?)

Stephanie gave me three options to call Vicki. One was her parents' place. (She had moved out?) Another was SEARS. She was working there and the third number was at her place. She had definitely moved out and found her own place. She'd be twenty-two now and on her own. Just like me.

My relationship with Joan was over, even if she didn't think so. I had changed so much from my old self, I was meeting new people, trying new things. My own life was progressing at a rapid rate and Joan seemed to be treading water.

When I reached her, Vicki sounded like her old self. Still an English lilt to her voice, still that laugh I liked. It would be interesting to see what she looked like given the differences time had made in her sister Stephanie.

The intervening seven years had altered both of us. I had dated other women so I felt I was on a different playing field meeting Vicki now. I could immediately see the changes in her too. She was no longer the skinny, nerdy teenager, now she was a very attractive, twenty-two-year-old. She still had that nose I liked. Her body had filled out too. I liked that. I could sense that she had had some experience with men. Was Wolfie still in the picture?

She was living with a girlfriend above a flower shop on Jarvis Street, which at the time, did not have the greatest reputation. Yet the CBC was located there. Having sold my car to Joan before moving to Toronto meant I had to take the TTC to see her. For wheels, Vicki was driving a station wagon she had rented from some friends while her beloved MG was stored away from that nasty, Toronto winter slush.

It was a Saturday when I met up with her and I had spent the day in a production meeting, discussing a student film we wanted to make about hang-gliding. Its working title was "Spirit of the Winds." We needed to come up with a dynamic presentation to convince our instructors to give us pricey film stock as well as the expensive processing it would need. Our teachers were all professionals and had heard lots of promises from other students so our sales pitch had to be topnotch.

While setting up our meeting on the phone, Vicki had asked me if I would, as a favour to her, photograph her face, specifically her nose. Apparently, she was going to have rhinoplasty and wanted some 'before' pictures. She trusted my photographic abilities enough to allow me to do it. Even after seven years, she hated having her photograph taken and I was the one guy she would allow herself to open up to have it done.

Now that I was studying with a professional photographic instructor (we had to take photography before we would be allowed to touch the expensive film cameras,) my skill and confidence level had increased dramatically from my high school days. Our instructor was a Czechoslovakian photographer named Ludi Dietrich and he would insist that in every photograph, there be an area, no matter how small of absolute black and another of absolute white in your photo. Otherwise, he would throw your photo assignment onto the floor and declare, "a piece of shit in the grass! Do it over again." Or if he didn't like your portraits, he would toss them aside and say, "passport picture!" and leave it at that. He was tough. And his disdain made me a better photographer. Years later, after we were married, Janet would tell me how she dropped out of his class because she couldn't stand his attitude.

Vicki was a more willing subject compared to the last time I had photographed her. Her having matured helped and the fact she trusted me worked in my favour. This time I used a tripod and a reflector to ensure a more professional result than the handheld stuff I had done of her in the past.

On meeting, we were more like old friends than old lovers. Mind you, technically, we had never been lovers. We had never had sex while we were dating. Lots of heavy petting but not the final act. She was too young? I was too inexperienced? The sex thing was not an issue here.

After the photo shoot, she offered to drive me home. This was a new experience for us as neither had owned a car in high school. In fact, I don't remember anyone driving to school in those days. The ride home was her way of saying thanks for taking her pictures.

Meeting again a week later to hand over the results of the shoot, I knew that the spark that had once existed between us had dimmed considerably and I could sense she felt the same way. We liked each other but both of us had changed so much in only seven years that we knew we would drift apart. When we parted, we knew that this was it for us. In my heart I wished her well and I could tell from her hug that she felt the same way.

Strangely, we hadn't even discussed the gift which was safe at my mother's home in London.

10 The Janet Sales Pitch

My roommate Bill and I stayed up all night convincing our fellow roommate Victor, to date a girl from the class a year ahead of us. Victor had mentioned to Bill and I that he was interested in a girl named Janet, that he liked her. But he was unsure about the whole thing.

First things first. We had to sell Victor on Janet so that he would pursue her, then we had to teach him how to actually ask her out. We spent a good portion of the night convincing and teaching him.

A week later, he proudly announces that he has asked Janet out. When we questioned him how he had done that, he described meeting late one night at the bus stop outside of Humber. After some idle chitchat, he asked her if she would like to go out with him sometime. Sometime? That's no way to ask a girl out. Sometime! To ask her out properly, it was necessary to have a specific date in mind or a specific event like a concert. Victor was crushed at our reaction. I don't think he ever asked her out again. I'll have to ask her. She is my wife after all.

The sales pitch we gave Victor must have lodged itself into my own brain. I began to pay attention to her. Mentally checking off all the same attributes we had described to Victor. She's attractive. Nice body. Has a great laugh. She's intelligent and easy to be with, etc.

Each student in third year was expected to direct an assigned film scene and we, as second years were delegated to working with them. I was often in Janet's vicinity, not that she paid me one scrap of attention. She was directing a scene from Shakespeare's Three Witches and her cameraman was an Italian guy named Angelo Constanzi. I was to be his assistant cameraman; loading film magazines, cleaning lenses or anything else he demanded. My being there was probably a good thing. Judging from the number of times he called out my name "Mack! Mack!" (his pronunciation,) to help him, I came to the realization that I knew more about shooting film than he did.

Watching Janet work with her friend Leslie, her assistant director, I tried to figure out this young woman. I had seen her once in the college's courtyard having a serious conversation with one of her classmates, Rocco Gismondi. I couldn't hear what they were saying but whatever it was, it looked deep. She had a locker not far away from mine, so I did get the odd chance to say hi or to talk about her film but I still wasn't feeling any real connection.

Janet didn't seem to mind being with me, yet we were never really alone; always surrounded by a group of friends. Our student union would hold pub nights and we got to enjoy famous bands in their early careers. Bands like Rough Trade, Lighthouse, and Crowbar. One Friday night, the Downchild Blues Band was playing. A large group of us were sitting and laughing together, enjoying their boisterous music. Pam, a girl in one of my electives, came by and asked me if I would like to dance. Janet's eyes followed us onto the dance floor. Many years later, she told me that was the moment she decided we should go out together. Who was this interloper, dancing with her guy? She let me chase her all over Humber until she caught me.

My ex-girlfriend, Joan, in a ploy to get back with me, loaned me her car while travelling out of the country. Since none of us had cars, she could park it in our space and save herself a hefty parking fee. Plus have a chance to connect with me.

I wasn't interested in Joan anymore but this gave me an opportunity to have a set of wheels for a fortnight. Janet was editing her "Witches" film after classes and I knew the last bus was at nine, so I would saunter into the edit suite around eight thirty or so. She would be engrossed in her editing and barely acknowledge my presence. That was okay. I had a plan.

I would casually mention that I had wheels now and if she wanted to stay later than nine, I could give her a ride home at nine thirty or ten. She always agreed. There were plenty of photo assignments to complete, so I'd spend that time in the darkroom. It was an ideal time to develop and print since almost all of the other students had gone home.

Every night, as I drove her home, I would let her know that I thought she was cute and that I wanted to go out with her. She listened sweetly to me yet never responded one way or the other. I was running out of time. In a few days, Joan would be returning and wanting her car back. In panic mode, I asked her if she would like to go with me to McDonalds the next night, (I wasn't going to be vague like Victor.) She said sure.

That first date was a schmozzle. Being a student on limited funds, I made her pay for her own meal. Afterwards, I invited her up to the apartment I was sharing with Bill and Victor. It was a seventeen-storey building located near the airport. We called it "The Dive at 265." The chocolate brown walls complemented the golden parquet flooring. A long balcony served as a launching pad for inflated condoms which we would drop to see whose would go the furthest.

Janet had mixed reactions to the place. She was impressed at its size and all the furnishings we had. But she couldn't stand the mould from the leaky ceiling. Her allergies flared up as soon as she entered the apartment. Even though my roommates and I had cleaned it meticulously on the chance she might visit that night.

The thing that made it a 'Dive' was that we were on the top floor and during the first spring we rented there, the roof began to leak. Water got under the parquet flooring, causing it to pop up randomly, meaning you couldn't open and close certain doors and cupboards. It got so bad that I went downtown and made a complaint to the Tenant's Advisory Board. An inspector came to look at the place and agreed that something had to be done.

After much prompting from the Tenant Board, the landlord came over. We told him to not bother taking off his galoshes since he would need them to walk through the place. Even though he could hear the squishing sound each footfall made, he said, "I don't hear nothing. There is no problem here."

He never did fix the place up but he must have received pressure from the inspector since he did give us the apartment directly below ours. A stairwell connected both front doors which gave us, as students, a six-bedroom apartment, with four bathrooms and two kitchens. When the inspector found out that the landlord had no intention of fixing our original place, he informed us that we didn't have to pay rent until it was fixed. For the last several months that I lived there, I didn't have to pay rent. I saved my money and it came in very handy in the spring of my third year.

We dated for several months, then Janet graduated. We weren't serious enough for me to attend her graduation ceremony and meet her parents. Janet was hired by CKVR in Barrie, just north of Toronto. She lived in a house that was divided up into three apartments. Hers was on the ground floor, at the back. Up above her was one of our Humber classmates, Mark who also worked at the station.

I visited Janet as often as I could on the weekends and we would party with Mark and others from CKVR. We all got along well. Mark was a cameraman at the station, shooting mostly commercials. I managed, in my third year, to secure a practicum there and go out with Mark on shoots. I discovered that Janet was operating a Bolex camera, shooting and editing short filler stories for the station, even though her real job was editing commercial breaks into the films the station broadcasted.

During my last year of college, Janet also came down to Toronto to visit, staying on the sixteenth floor at the 'Dive.' That apartment was nice and dry and there wasn't any mould to bother her allergies. It was on one of these visits that I let her know that I was moving to Edmonton, Alberta, in western Canada, where I had accepted a job as a news film cameraman. Neither of us knew at the time what this meant for our relationship or that this was not to become our final goodbye.

11 Siberia With Jobs

My best clothes. That's what I should wear on my first plane ride. Only rich people flew, right? So, I had better look my best. My ensemble consisted of blue tweed pants, a brown jacket over a dress shirt that had a faint checked design in green thread, under a brown sweater vest. Rounding off my outfit was a dark blue knitted tie. This was my favourite outfit.

Much to my shock and surprise when I boarded the flight to Edmonton, I discovered that the airplane was full of a tough-looking crowd; mostly men wearing torn T-shirts and grease-stained jeans. What kind of place was this that I was going to?

In all my twenty-five years, I had never been outside Ontario except for a couple of trips to Michigan, just across the St. Clair River from Mooretown. Both times I was accompanied by my brother and father. We went to see the Clyde Beatty and Cole Brothers Circus, (where I decided to become a sword swallower,) and the second time was to see the movie, "Grand Prix" at a downtown Detroit cinema.

When my family learned that I had accepted a job in Edmonton, their reaction was, "why would you want to go there? It's Siberia with jobs!"

Coming from an English background, I am one to take things literally. When the plane came in for a landing at Edmonton, I curiously peered out my window. I expected to see the kinds of vehicles described in a book our father had read to us when we were small. It was titled "The Long Walk" and recounted the true story of a group of prisoners who escaped the Russian Gulag and walked all the way to India.

The heavy-duty vehicles the Russians used at the prison camp had a tall, cylindrical gas generator behind the driver's compartment. The fuel was wood, it burned birch or ash, both being in plentiful supply. The trucks themselves looked like something from the around World War One.

As the plane descended, I could make out individual vehicles. "Why there is a Chevy! Here comes a Ford. Their cars and trucks look just like the ones in Ontario!" I thought to myself. Even the bus I entered that would take me to downtown Edmonton looked exactly like the busses I was familiar with. This place didn't look like Siberia.

Edmonton's river valley stunned me. As the airport bus ground its way up a steep hill, I was captivated by a castle-like building crowning the top of the valley. Wow! What is this beautiful place?

In fact, the bus stopped at that castle which turned out to be the MacDonald Hotel, an old railway hotel. I gathered my things to trudge my way to the YMCA, just blocks away. I wondered why I was getting such strange looks from passers-by. I had a pair of antique wooden cross-country skis over my right shoulder and a suitcase in my left hand. I had sent most of my stuff (including Vicki's Christmas gift,) in a trunk to CFRN, the station where I would be working.

It was March nineteenth and it still looked like winter here in this prairie city. Snow still clung to curbs and was piled in windrows down the streets. It looked like I might use those skis after all.

That first night in Edmonton everything felt strange. I had eaten my supper at the downtown Woolworth's lunch counter and then retreated to my cell-like room. It was bare of any familiar mementos; the bed was hard and I felt totally alone. Yet I still had the thrill of excitement realizing my dream of becoming a news film cameraman that would begin on the morrow.

With months to go before graduating from Humber, I had sent out sixty cover letters and resumes to every TV station in the country. I heard back right away from CBC Yellowknife that they were interested but I decided to pass as the idea of moving way up north was beyond my comfort zone.

One day, I received a call at the 'Dive' from the secretary to the General Manager from CFRN Television in Edmonton. The lady told me that Mr. Alloway, was going to be in Toronto the very next week and would I be able to meet with him? Just to point out the arrogance of my youth, I declined, explaining to her that I had a shoot that day and couldn't change it. She seemed unperturbed and mentioned that the news director, Bruce Hogle, was going to be in Toronto for a Radio and Television News Director Association meeting in two weeks. Would I be able to meet him? I agreed to that request.

It was a Friday afternoon that I met Bruce Hogle at a downtown hotel. Bruce explained to me that the Commonwealth Games were coming to Edmonton and the station needed skilled people they could put to work right away with a minimum of training. It looked to him that I could do that. From my demo reel, he liked a story I had done about cab drivers protesting at Toronto City Hall. They were upset with city council not allowing them to place protective shields between themselves and their passengers.

He also like a story I had created from still photographs of a young woman being arrested for taking all her clothes off in the fountain at Nathan Phillips Square. I had the whole episode recorded from her stripping down to her being escorted away from the square, a blanket covering her nakedness.

After an hour of chatting, Bruce stood up, stuck out his hand and when I shook it, he said, "you're hired!" I was shocked. What had I just agreed to? The only thing I knew about Edmonton came from the Pontiac Parisienne I had owned that had come from there. My brother-in-law Paul came with me to inspect it before buying it. We lifted up the hood and wondered what all the extra cables and wires were for. There were cords hanging out of the grill: the battery had an electric blanket around it, we traced another cord back to the engine block, then a third one to a small heater inside the passenger compartment. A block heater? A battery warmer? An in-car heater? What kind of place was this?

I knew about block heaters. We owned a car in Mooretown that had one. My mother had driven away from our house many times without unplugging it. We would find pieces of copper wire and electrical cord scattered along Emily Street, marking Mom's path much like dropping bread crumbs to find her way home. The old man was pissed whenever this happened.

To get to the station from downtown it was necessary to take a cab as there was no bus service to the western edge of the city. A transit bus would only have taken me to Jasper Place, leaving me with a twenty-eight-block walk along a very busy road that had no sidewalks, to get to my destination.

The cabbie must have been mistaken. He let me out in front of a motel. A totem pole stood guard outside the building. Walking into the lobby confirmed that I was in the wrong place. Knotty pine paneling covered the walls. The reception desk had upright pine planks curving around it. I expected a bellhop to come and take my bag. This was Sunwapta Broadcasting. Home of Sunwapta Sam. I was, after all, in the right place.

The friendly receptionist buzzed Bruce to come out and meet me. I hadn't seen him since our interview in Toronto and I felt less adrift seeing a familiar face. My career as a news film cameraman had begun.

We negotiated our way around the sprawling complex. The station had grown with the popularity of television and additions had been tacked on in a helter-skelter fashion. There were countless stairs to go up and down; we threaded our way through narrow corridors until we reached the basement where the photography department was located. Bruce introduced me to my new boss, Walter, and his right-hand man Diet (pronounced Deet) and a wiry Dutch cameraman named Marinus.

Just as soon a Bruce departed, Walter showed me the photography studio where I would be expected to take pictures and then process them in the darkroom next door. It was at that point that Walter told me he didn't like me and never would have hired me. What a welcome! This news was shocking. My jaw dropped. I had cut all ties to home, left my girlfriend behind, and travelled to this place where I knew no one, only to find out that I wasn't wanted here. What a great start to my new career! "I've made a big mistake," I told myself.

Still standing stupefied as Walter left the room, I wondered what lay in store for me when Diet entered the room. Was he the axe man? Diet directed me to the darkroom and no sooner had the inner door closed, he said to me, "don't listen to that guy. He's just mad that Bruce hired you and not himself. I'm sure if Bruce thinks you are a good cameraman, you'll work out fine here."

This was reassuring. When Walter had left me standing in the photo studio, I started to calculate how much money I had and figured I could stick this place out for two weeks and then go back to Ontario with my tail between my legs. Yet this older cameraman seemed to have some faith in me. I decided to stay put.

I owe my career to this swell Dutchman. He helped me find an apartment, he loaded my trunk which I had shipped to the station into his own car, ("we wondered whose trunk this was,") and introduced me to his family, even inviting me over to his home for meals once I had a car.

Before boarding the plane to Edmonton, I had decided that since I knew no one in Alberta, I would use my legal first name, Adrian, even though I had been called Mike for my first twenty-five years.

It all started with my parents as new immigrants wanting to fit in. Before my pregnant mother had arrived from England with two little girls in hand, it had been suggested to my father that he trim his walrus moustache and cut his hair shorter. My father obliged even if that meant that my mother didn't recognize him when they finally met at Union Station in Toronto.

Once settled in their new home, my mother having given birth to my twin and I, my parents were told that they couldn't call me Adrian. That was a girl's name. They yielded and started calling me Mike, (or Michael when I was in trouble.) Besides, calling the twins Chris and Mike rolled off the tongue much more easily than Chris and Adrian.

I soon discovered that there was a great need here in this province for trained and experienced television people. I called Janet who was still working at CKVR to get out here ASAP. Not only was I missing her, but I was confident she could get a job recording sound here right away. Sound recording was her area of expertise and she could do better than working at a tiny station. This was a major market even if they might not have thought so in Ontario.

Janet arrived mid-week and by Friday, she was going to interviews. One of them, Access Alberta, offered her a sound recording and mixing position to start the following Tuesday, after the long weekend. She accepted. She would be working on educational programming for Alberta schools.

I must have proven something to Walter because within a year, I was shooting out-of-town assignments and filming documentaries in San Francisco, Seattle and Toronto. This was the big time! I was a successful news film cameraman.

A year later, I was approached by the CTV News reporter, Robert Hurst. I had developed a friendship with his cameraman, Bruce Murphy. Hurst came to me to say, "my cameraman doesn't want to work on the weekends. Would you be interested in being on call?" I was flattered that the National News would think I had the skills to shoot for them.

All summer long, I wore a pager on the weekends and never ventured far from town, waiting for a message. Robert never did call on me that summer. However, one night in the early fall, I was working the afternoon shift, three until eleven, when the newsroom heard about a pipeline explosion in Central Alberta. No reporters were available, so our late news anchor, Rick Brown and I drove down. The accident had happened east of Red Deer (the halfway point between Edmonton and Calgary.) We were kept well back from the scene yet I still managed to get film of the monstrous flames. I noticed the CTV crew were there too. We all stayed in the same hotel that night.

The next morning, there was a mine collapse in Hinton. We huddled. Rick had to be back for his newscast and the CTV guys decided that Murphy should go with Rick back to Edmonton. Hurst knew that Murphy could sneak onto the mine property and get exclusive footage. I was to stay with Hurst and do the National story which involved interviews, standups and driving to Calgary where I was to process the film and edit the piece. I hadn't edited since Humber College. I was nervous yet super excited.

Shortly thereafter, Murphy accepted a posting to China and I was offered his job. Hurst must have been pleased with my work. It was difficult to tell Bruce Hogle that I was leaving but he took it gracefully. I think he was proud of my promotion and felt it reflected well on him and the station. Besides, not only would I be in the same building, I would be working for the same network.

12 Equipage

I was over the moon to be a CTV news cameraman. Little did I realize how much I would learn in the next few years and how hard I would need to work.

Robert Hurst taught me to be aggressive. When he left to go to Ottawa, Bob Evans who replaced him taught me writing to visuals and feature storytelling. He was replaced by Mark Sikstrom; when he first met Brent the soundman and myself, his reaction was "not you guys!"

Oh No! It looked as though our mangy, Heinz 57 puppy Jeep, was going to launch himself into the freezing waters of Maligne Lake, high up in the mountains above Jasper. As if we didn't have enough to contend with. We had been zig-zagging all morning from one side of the mountain lake to the other in our cedar strip canoe. We were supposed to be paddling in a straight line, following Robert Hurst and his wife Cathy and now they were paddling further and further away from us.

We had adopted Jeep (named after Popeye's dog) when a neighbour was moving away and didn't want him anymore. He wasn't paper trained, couldn't heel when out for a walk or sleep in his own bed. Only ours would do. You couldn't describe him as handsome either. I guess that's why we loved him. He was, pardon the pun, the underdog.

Janet was growing increasingly frustrated with my inept paddling. She had been a competitive canoeist and I had never been in a canoe before. Plus, I was going through withdrawal from having left my smokes back in the car. A cigarette right then would have calmed my nerves but done nothing for my aerobic conditioning. I was going to need all the aerobic capacity I could muster if we were going to reach the end of the lake, fourteen miles distant with all three of us safely in the canoe.

Pulling the dog back into the canoe caused it to tip precariously close to the blue green glacial waters of the lake. We both had life jackets on but neither of us was a particularly good swimmer and we doubted Jeep, with his questionable heritage, would fare well in the frigid water.

Hundreds of paddle strokes later, the skies clouded over and the calm lake surface became increasingly choppy. The Hurst's' had beached their canoe onto the far shore, only halfway to our destination. Once we cut across the waves, dog intact, we joined them to discuss our plans. It looked like the storm was worsening and we would have to camp here, right next to the 'No Camping' sign.

We were glad that night that Jeep wanted to sleep with us. It was like having a living hot water bottle in bed that stayed warm until morning. The storm lessened in the night but we decided to canoe back to our starting point since the lake was still rough and we would be paddling into the wind. The Hurst's had probably taken into consideration my lack of canoeing prowess and thought it wiser to go back. Janet felt the same way.

On the way back, a Parks Canada motor launch hailed us and we hove to in the middle of the lake. Since Robert and Cathy were in the lead, they spoke to the wardens who were most displeased with us having camped in a day use area. Robert used all his considerable charm and talked them out of giving us a ticket or worse, having to board their craft with our canoes in tow.

While working with Hurst I got my introduction to Electronic News Gathering. Being an ambitious reporter, he wanted us to be the first ENG crew for CTV News. Video was the coming thing and had the promise of being more efficient than film. That was the selling feature that Hurst used to convince Toronto that we should switch over. Toronto said we could try it.

More efficient? The technology was so new that we could only rent gear from a production company and I was convinced they had taken advantage of us by renting us their derelict equipment. Jack, their technician tried his best to teach me the fundamentals of video production. Not wanting to appear stupid, I just nodded and smiled at all the technical gibberish he was spouting: frame rates, zebra patterns, tube registering, white balancing. Zebra patterns? Weren't they an English crosswalk? Tubes? What the hell were tubes?

From a practical point of view, using the gear was even worse. The camera only shot the video. I was used to my old news film camera that exposed the image and recorded the audio at the same time. With this newfangled electronic gear, to record the video and the audio at the same time, it was necessary for me to wear a junction box around my waist. A thick cable led to the tape deck and a thinner cable led to the camera. I needed to switch on the tape deck first then the camera. I was not only a shooter, but now I was a cable wrangler. I should call my union rep and protest. Wait a minute, we weren't unionized.

Every night I sweated over the equipment; tightening screws, gaffer-taping parts together, hoping it wouldn't all fall apart on the next day's shoot. Whenever we were at the production company where we had rented the equipment, I would give a bunch of leftover screws to Jack and tell him to fix the stuff. Years later Jack and I worked for the same company. He told me that after he had fixed the gear, he would be left with a handful of screws too! Is it any wonder I had so many problems with it?

I was very close to quitting. I didn't know what I was doing and I had no confidence that the video I was shooting would even be useable. The quality of the video was worse than VHS. Any bright lights in the frame would cause long smears to obscure the subject. The camera wouldn't white balance at night under the salmon-coloured glow of the Edmonton street lights. The tape-recording heads would clog with magnetic dust which would necessitate ejecting the tape and using a long, specially designed Q-Tip dabbed in alcohol to clean the residue off the recording heads.

Getting our stories to air was a complicated process (no efficiency here) of driving to the production company, recording Robert's voice-over in my car after he had written the script, having an editor edit the piece on 3/4-inch tape and then having someone else transfer it to 1-inch tape. Then it was a race to CFRN where a whole production crew was standing by, waiting for us to feed the item by satellite to Toronto. The station didn't have 3/4-inch capabilities at the time, and it was necessary to use their mobile unit, equipped with a 1-inch machine, and roll tape from there. Our feed time was seven-twenty in the evening and we had the satellite for five minutes. That meant that if everything was copacetic then we had time to send the story to headquarters over only two tries.

At the time, there was a lot of animosity between the government of Alberta and the federal government, located in Ottawa. We often had the lead story which meant staying later and feeding live to the show in Toronto. There could be no mistakes. Lloyd Robertson wouldn't tolerate any. Nor would the executive producer and on down the line. With all the steps required to produce a ninety second story, the possibility for failure was quite high. This was one more reason to consider quitting and going back to film.

In the short time I worked with Robert he taught me to be more aggressive and to push the boundaries of my comfort level. I was becoming a better news cameraman. I was sad to see him leave and I wondered who Toronto would replace him with. Another canoeist perhaps?

"Now Adrian, I want you to stand in line and call me when you get to the front." In our household we still jokingly refer to this quote whenever one of us has to queue anywhere. This new Alberta Bureau chief wasn't one to stand in line when he could get me, the younger and more junior member of the team to do it for him. We were picking up accreditation to film a ski event in Calgary and the lineup was long.

Bob Evans was happiest when perusing the newspaper, puffing away on a cigar, looking for feature story ideas he could pitch to the assignment desk in Toronto. I was still geared up to shoot hard news the way Robert Hurst had taught me and I didn't grasp Bob's talent at matching words with pictures. I only now wish I had been more mature so that I could learn how to write from Mr. Evans, especially now that I am professing to be a writer.

Bob was a wonderful guy to work with, I never saw him get mad or aggressive. He could get a little perturbed perhaps when the assignment desk in Toronto was making questionable calls or what he thought were unreasonable demands.

Our one on-going dispute was over my van. Bob was not pleased with my choice of vehicle that was required for our work; an old silver cargo van. What's wrong with that you ask? There were three of us on the crew, now that we had a soundman-editor named Brent, working with us. But there were only two seats in the vehicle. The third person, usually Bob, had to sit in the back atop a gear case. Or perhaps it was the bright red roosters on each side of the van that he didn't like. We were turned away from media parking at several news events while we watched our competitors from the CBC waltz through the barricades in their bureau car, emblazoned with the CBC's exploding pizza logo.

My choosing this van could have been a hold-over from my days at CFRN, where for the first year I was there, we had to provide our own vehicles. One cameraman, as a way of protesting, would show up with the worst beaters he could find, then stop underneath the station owner's office window and rev the engine. Blue-black clouds of burning oil would drift through the open window into Dr. Rice's office. Reporters complained about his vehicles. One had huge holes in the floorboards where snow, ice and rain would fly up into the interior of the car. Their clothing would be soaked and, in some cases, ruined. Most of them refused to work with him.

Coming from Eastern Canada, Bob loved the romance of the west. Cowboys, ranches the size of townships and of course, the Rocky Mountains. He was tickled by the names of places too. We shot a Christmas story about purchasing a license to travel deep into the forest outside of Edmonton and cut down your own Christmas tree. In his standup, while he sawed away at the tree, he took great delight in signing off with "Bob Evans, CTV News, Carrot Creek, Alberta."

Some of my most visual stories were with him. Like the time we covered Canada's first paraplegic skydiver. To see this individual tumble into the sky and land in Pigeon Lake, three thousand feet below, was pure television magic. Or the time we did a story on the Wagner Bog. Who knew that orchids grew in Central Alberta?

Bob Evans totally saved my butt one evening a couple of weeks before Christmas in 1981. Janet and I were having dinner with our good friends Bill and Sue Purchase. We had all known each other since our days at Humber College. Bill was now a cameraman at CFRN. On that particular evening, I had turned my pager off, being sick and tired of being on call all the time. I had begun to understand Robert Hurst's comment about his cameraman not wanting to work on the weekends.

On our way home, listening to the radio in the car, we were shocked to hear that an airplane had crashed into an Edmonton Hospital. That definitely was national news!

At that time, Edmonton had a municipal airport just north of downtown and aircraft as large as 737s would land on its short runways. Very close to that airport was the Royal Alexandra Hospital, a central city hospital sitting right on the flight path. It was always a surprise to come out of the hospital and be startled by the screaming of jet engines while a monstrous plane passed overhead, seemingly about to hit the hospital. This time one did.

The accident involved a small airplane with a pilot and one passenger, coming in from Fort McMurray. The weather was clear but cold, it being December. The plane crashed into the top floor of the hospital, luckily, at the time that floor was vacant. Still, patients on lower floors had to be evacuated due to the risk of spilled aviation fuel igniting. The pilot died from his injuries and the passenger was taken to another hospital where he recovered.

I knew at that moment that I was in deep trouble. I hurriedly called Bob when I got home and learned to my relief that he and Brent had pieced together a story from CFRN footage. Our bosses in Toronto were very angry that I had been unavailable and chewed me out severely. Bob covered for me by telling them the equipment was in for repairs when the accident happened and that got me off the hook. It was their equipment and their responsibility. I owed him.

it was as though the Alberta Bureau was a way-station for CTV News. I was in a stable and loving relationship and liked Edmonton. Why move anywhere else? Hurst had left to go to Washington and now Evans was being assigned to Ottawa. This meant that Brent and I would have to break in a new reporter. We had heard through the grapevine that it was going to be a CBC reporter from Calgary; a guy we had seen on and off covering news in that fair city.

We got off to a rocky start. On his first story, during his standup, he wanted me to zoom out from a sign and onto him. I refused. "I don't zoom. That's what local stations do." We argued and I relented. He was the Bureau Chief. Although, he must have heard something about it from Toronto as he never asked for such a thing again.

Mark really put Edmonton on the map as far as CTV News was concerned. We covered stories from the North pole to the Gulf of Mexico together. He took a hard news stand and that sometimes got us into hot water, especially with the Prime Minister's security detail.

The three of us, the reporter, sound-man and myself were running from a hotel ballroom in Lethbridge, Alberta, where we had just shot a press conference with the Prime Minister, Pierre Trudeau. You could say the assignment desk in Toronto had sent us out on a "death watch" as Trudeau was intensely disliked here in Western Canada. Just months before, he had taken the train from Vancouver to Calgary and it was pelted with rotten fruit in British Columbia. The public was not impressed with Trudeau's "Salmon Arm Salute" either, something we had caught on camera and that was flashed around the globe.

After the press conference, we heard that Trudeau was planning on confronting protestors outside the hotel. This could be good. We had to get it. But how do we get there before he does? The Prime Minister has a crack security team and they are trained to hustle their charge through any number of scenarios.

One of us remembered from a previous news conference that a service corridor ran underneath the hotel that could bring us out into the parking lot where the protestors were gathered. In a situation like this, the cameraman is in the lead so that they can capture immediately whatever might transpire. Second in line is the sound-man since you need audio to go with the video. The reporter comes up last.

We pelted down the corridor turning our heads every now and then to see if Trudeau was following us. If we saw him, that would ensure we got to the parking lot ahead of him. We kept running. Do we go this way down this hall to our right? What about the one up ahead? That one? It was while all three of had turned our heads to check behind us that SMACK! I ran right into the Prime Minister, who was running towards us. We had been going the wrong way.

"Oh no. Not you guys again!" He says upon seeing who has slammed right into him and his detail. After quick apologies and being roughly man-handled aside, the entourage streamed down the very hallway we had come from. Following the group, we knew we were headed in the right direction. I'd just have to roll the camera as Trudeau's entourage barged out of the hotel and into the parking lot.

His response on recognizing us had everything to do with his previous train ride. We had boarded the train in Vancouver around six o'clock on a Friday evening. Lugging our suitcases and camera gear, we were disgusted to find out that we had been relegated to one of the last cars on a very long train. Trudeau's private car was very close to the front.

Our job was to get out at each stop and record the Prime Minister greeting constituents. That meant we would spend the whole night constantly dashing up to the front of the train, to shoot whatever transpired and racing even faster back to our car before the train left the station without us.

After a couple of stops where nothing happened, the train settled into a long journey through the night. The sky was clear with a very bright moon, we had incredible views from the observation car where we camped once darkness fell. It was deserted and we had it all to ourselves. I particularly remember one vista as the train traversed a long curve, there were white rapids on rushing rivers with a glimpse the engine far ahead of us.

We stayed up all night in case something happened. Around ten the next morning, the train pulled into Salmon Arm. There was word that the train had been pelted in the night with rotten fruit to show the discord British Columbians felt toward the Liberal Prime Minister. If true, this was getting exciting! Protestors lined the station platform. Trudeau did not make an appearance. His young sons were travelling with him and their heads were looking out his window from behind the curtain. Suddenly they left and an arm was seen to rise between the drape and the glass. The hand formed a bird.

We ran to our car at the back of the train. Immediately, we played the footage back. "Do we have it?" the reporter asks. "There it is. You can clearly see him giving the finger!" I tell him. I rewind it and let it play for him. We couldn't see Trudeau's face but we could see those huge biceps stretching his t-shirt, a white t-shirt with a red band hemming the sleeve. "It's got to be him," says the reporter.

We'll have to get out at the next stop to confirm it. If it is him, this footage is dynamite!" Even our jaded reporter was getting excited.

The next stop was Sycamous where once again we ran to the front of the train. Trudeau was just stepping out onto the platform of his car and waving to the small crowd there. Sure enough, he was wearing a white t-shirt with red piping on the ends of the sleeves. We had him. The Prime Minister giving the finger to protestors. The reporter ran to a payphone in the station to call the assignment desk. After making sure the reporter was confident that the footage showed the Prime Minister giving "the Fuddle Finger of Fate," they instructed him to have the sound-man stay behind in Sycamous and they would send a helicopter to pick him and the footage up and whisk them to Calgary where it could be fed by satellite to Toronto.

We didn't see Trudeau for some time after that until running into him in Lethbridge. Our next brush with him was when he was touring the double tracking that CN Rail had just completed.

The thing about media tours is that on one hand, you get opportunities at footage you wouldn't otherwise get. The downside is that you are at the mercy of the organizers of the tour. You see what they want you to see. Often, you find out that your competition is going so you have no choice but to go along too. Such was the case when CN Rail wanted the Prime Minister to see the work that had been done to the rail system between Edmonton and Vancouver. At great expense and with a lot of government help, the rail giant had doubled the tracking so that more than twice the rail traffic could be shipped westward.

The media was herded through a rear cargo ramp onto a giant Chinook helicopter that would shuttle us to Jasper where the tour was to start. Inside the giant craft were two rows of seats lining the inside walls. Everyone's gear was stuffed in the middle between us. We should have known how uncomfortable and noisy a ride it would be when each person was handed a set of headphone-like sound protectors. The seats were made of a military-type webbing and offered simply a place to settle your butt, comfort be damned.

We vibrated and shook for two hours. Roughly half the time it would have taken to drive. One advantage was that our flight path followed Highway 16, which meant I would have a brief opportunity to photograph our acreage. I was convinced that at three thousand feet I would be able to see it or the area around it from four miles distant. The chopper was shaking so hard that I couldn't hold my still camera steady enough to get the shot. Still, it did look pretty from so high up.

Just as soon as we landed, we were hustled aboard a special CN train that had an observation car hitched to its rear. Trudeau could sit there in comfort and watch the twin rails appear beneath his feet and slowly join together in a distant perspective. An amplified voice described the many features of the new system while we watched from the sidelines. A couple of wide shots showing the PM sitting with his back to us seemed to be all we were going to get.

Having been distracted by the mountain scenery, I turned and saw that Herb Tyler, the CBC National cameraman had somehow positioned himself in front of Trudeau and was getting a reaction shot (just as boring as the back of the Prime Minister's head.) Hey! What the heck? I thought we weren't allowed to get anywhere near the big man! Right away Mark was on the PM's press aid complaining. How could the CBC (he called it the Canadian Broadcorping Castration) get a shot and not us? He whined enough that Brent and I were allowed to get one shot of the PM trying to look interested at the four steel rails unravelling in front of him.

The train stopped and we were allowed to scrum Trudeau and quickly shoot some B-Roll before scrambling back on the train. It brought back memories of covering his fateful train trip where he gave the "Fuddle Finger of Fate" to Salmon Arm.

At the end of the day, tired from an early start and a boring trip, we jumped off the train, glad to be through. Sikstrom wanted a shot of the PM walking away from the train a short distance to an awaiting, but smaller helicopter. Then he wanted to ask the PM one more question. Really? These national reporters just love an opportunity to be in the company of someone as high ranking as the Prime Minister. We couldn't believe that we would have to gear up yet again just so the reporter could be a big shot and ask Trudeau a question by himself. Our competition had already packed up and were ready to board the bus that would take us back to the Chinook for a noisy and uncomfortable flight back to Edmonton.

The technique of walking backward (backpedaling) and interviewing involves the sound man grabbing the cameraman by the belt and pulling him backwards while he is walking forward. Add to this the fact that the sound man and cameraman are joined together by an umbilical cord which binds them together. To make matters more difficult, the sound man is also holding a long boom pole and trying his best to aim the shotgun microphone toward the subject's mouth.

We had never tried this before and we were shaky at best. The PM wasn't going to wait for us to be absolutely ready and he continued walking with his phalanx of security and toadies surrounding him. As we neared Trudeau's helicopter, Sikstrom managed to ask his "important" question. Before the Prime Minister could answer, Brent (in the lead,) stumbles into a coil of rusted wire. I tumble backward into him. The boom pole which Brent had placed lower to the ground so the mic would be facing up toward the Prime Minister's mouth quickly flew up to the PM's crotch. His security men immediately jumped into action. Two of them closed ranks with him and two more grabbed Brent and I and threw us to the ground. All four men then converged on Trudeau who they hustled into the chopper, it's long blades already turning.

As we got to our feet, his helicopter lifted off and quickly banked away from the scene. "What the hell happened here?" Sikstrom wants to know. We are all embarrassed. The CBC crew, watching from the tour bus windows, couldn't contain their glee and laughter as we boarded the bus.

We had the last laugh though when we got back to Edmonton and played the footage on our edit suite. Jogging the tape back and forth, we could see the boom and mic slowly ascend towards the Prime minister's crotch, inches away from a serious incident. Then the footage careens wildly as we fall to the ground. That was the time we almost nutted Trudeau. No wonder he was dismayed to see us again.

When I meet people and tell them I was news cameraman they often ask if I ran into famous people. I can answer them, yes, I did.

13 Family Time

Janet and I were married in our apartment on Thanksgiving weekend, 1980. It was in a place called Green Tree Village although the complex was surrounded by flat, brown lawns and stunted, dried up saplings. Hardly a village. And certainly, there were no green trees. We only invited close friends and later phoned our families to say: "guess what we did this morning?"

In the rush to get to our apartment on time, one of Janet's bridesmaids gave another driver the finger as he cut her off while entering our parking lot. Little did she know the driver was the Justice of the Peace and that within minutes, she would have to stand facing him. His name was Sam Mc Gee (as in the famous poem,) and because of his advanced age, he couldn't tell which bridesmaid had so rudely gestured at him. The two of them were dressed alike so he just glowered at both of them.

Janet is from a family of seven children, five of them being girls. Her dad, in his glee at not having to pay for another wedding, sent us a cheque to buy ourselves a brand-new washer and dryer.

My family wanted to do something special for us. My sister Hilary phoned me to find out about our décor. At the time, there wasn't much of it. We had an old cast-off couch and chair from a friend's mother, given to us because even Goodwill did not want it. We were using Janet' sewing machine table for our meals, and my old trunk as a dresser. My family pooled their money and bought us each a dresser, a tall boy for me and a long many drawered one for Janet. They were made of solid wood in a light maple finish. They're still kicking around somewhere in the basement.

My mom once described Janet and I as being two peas from the same pod. We like a lot of the same things, share books and music, enjoy being out in nature, we have similar political views. Both of us are twins; perhaps that special bond we both shared with our siblings makes it easier for us to compromise and adapt in a paired relationship. We have had a very happy marriage.

Soon after marrying, we found the apartment too confining and we bought a five-acre parcel of land that had an eight hundred square foot house on it, about twenty minutes west of the city. I was working with Mark Sikstrom at the time and he nicknamed the place "Brown Acres." We thought we had lucked out when we discovered that the place also came with a Ford tractor that could be used in the summer to cut the three acres of grass and in the winter to plough the three-hundred-foot-long driveway.

Janet was working as a sound recordist and mixer for Access Alberta, a provincially funded production house that made programs for the Alberta Department of Education. It was just up the road from CFRN, where our offices were located. At the time, our western friends found a twenty-minute commute too long and were astounded by our purchase. Coming from eastern Canada, where commutes are longer, we never gave it a second thought.

A few years later, we decided to start a family. Our son was born in 1984. It had been a difficult pregnancy and we never picked out names for the baby. While Janet was resting, the nurses pressured me to fill in the birth registry. I came up with Christopher Frederick, the first name after my twin and the second after Janet's brother, who had recently died. Janet insisted we call him Christopher to distinguish him from his uncle. That lasted until kindergarten, when his teacher re-named him Chris. Our boy was happy with the change and Janet acquiesced. Within the family, Chris, now a grown man of six feet, is known as Little Chris, and his uncle, the same height as me, (five foot and five inches tall,) is known as Big Chris.

The day he was born, with Janet settled in a room, I came and sat with her. She gave me the baby to hold and I rocked him in my arms, walking about the room. Finally, the nurse came by and suggested I let the new mother and baby sleep. I handed him over to Janet and realized the front of my shirt was soaked. Riding the elevator down to the main floor with doctors, hospital workers and other visitors, I proudly stuck out my chest, my wet shirt a testimony to the fact that I now had a son.

Although always at the ninety percentiles for height and weight, Chris had a rough beginning to life; he was asthmatic with many food allergies. Many a time we rushed him to the hospital where they would put him on oxygen and send us home with puffers and pills. With a bright and sunny, fun-loving disposition those set-backs did not get the better of him and he was a mischievous boy who loved playing with his Duplo and creating fantasy worlds for himself and his friends.

Today, when my son and I travel together, we like to play pranks on each other; harmless, almost adolescent in their silliness. Such as filling the toes of the other person's shoes with rolled up socks. Or taking odd photos with their phone when they aren't looking. Switching sugar for salt. Stupid stuff.

We often do a bikepacking trip for a week every summer and the outdoors offers great opportunities for pranks.

While on one such trip, as we pedaled across a field, up ahead Chris stops and when I catch up to him he tells me he sees dark shapes up ahead on the trail. He tells me they are bears. We had already seen many and had our bear spray canisters attached to our handlebars, at the ready for use. As we carefully approached, I pulled out my bear spray at the ready, I could see that they weren't bears, they were cows, he was just pranking me. There was a mother and a small herd of calves blocking the trail. Cows! Yikes, I didn't know what to do. They didn't scare me the way bears do however, I remember from my childhood, growing up in the country, that cows can be very unpredictable.

Coming toward us from the other direction is another cyclist who simply rides into the group of livestock and slaps their rear ends causing them to scatter, leaving him room to maneuver around them. Chris and I give each other a look that says, "let's go while we can!"

Cautiously threading our bikes through the pack is not enough. The calves, already nervous, begin to panic and charge up the narrow trail. Chris' strength has put him in the lead which means that I am stuck with the calves in front of me and the mother cow behind me. Clods of dirt are being thrown up from the rampaging animals, coating my sunglasses, making it hard to see where I am cycling. I can't get ahead of them.

"Dad! That mother cow is right on your butt!" Chris shouts back at me, glancing over his shoulder. I look through my dirty lenses and see the writing on my mirror, "Objects in the mirror are closer than they appear," No shit. On closer inspection, I can see that my mirror is completely full of one raging cow. She is moments away from ramming right into me. I am pedaling for all I am worth.

What saves me is the calves suddenly turn to the left to barge down a side trail and the angry mother follows them. Chris and I pull to a stop, breathing hard. "Maybe you shouldn't be listening to your IPOD?" he asks. "I had to shout several times before you heard me! I thought you were a goner, Dad!" Even though he was upset by the incident, I was silently pleased: my son always has my back.

We were bikepacking the Slocan Rail Trail, north of Castlegar, British Columbia. The year before we had found the trail by accident on our way home from a disappointing trip along the Kettle Valley Railway Trail. The KVR was in a horrible state from all the motorized vehicles using it as a backwoods freeway. With a little research, we discovered that in the Slocan Valley, there is a culture that frowns upon using motorized machines on this abandoned railbed.

Later, over a beer at our campsite, celebrating our escape from the mad cow, I marvel at my son. What a fine man he has turned out to be. He runs his own successful business and has worked at creating a good life for himself in Saskatoon. I credit his mother for doing such a great job of raising him. Maybe I taught him to weight lift and how to enjoy the outdoors.

He is quite a physical specimen. Towering over me at six feet tall and two hundred and forty-five pounds, mostly firm muscle, he has a long red beard that cascades down to his chest, (he calls himself Red Beard Viking,) and long strawberry blonde hair down to the middle of his back. Like me, he was always shy around women and he found that female strangers would come up to him and ask to touch his hair. He had inadvertently discovered an easy way to break the ice with the fairer sex.

I see a lot of my father in him. There is a picture of my Dad in Burma during the war. He is wearing an Australian bush hat with one side turned up tilted at a jaunty angle, a straight-stemmed pipe jutting from the corner of his mouth. He looks up and to his right as though wondering what his future might hold.

When the Boy (a term of endearment that my wife and I use when talking about him) was nineteen, he was the spitting image of his grandfather at that age. I begged him to let me recreate the photo. It would have involved him shaving off his beard and moustache, tying his long hair up and somehow hiding it under an Australian bush hat that I have. Hmmm. No wonder he didn't want to do it. That's a lot to ask for one picture from a teenage boy.

There was a time when we thought we were going to lose him. He became ill and after a week of lying in bed, Janet went to help him up to the washroom. He collapsed after a few feet and because of his size, she couldn't support his weight. They both fell to the floor, a glass of water Janet was holding smashing into fragments, water everywhere. When the paramedics arrived, they were suspicious of the circumstances. A man lying on the floor, broken glass surrounding him, a liquid soaking his clothing. "What is going on here?" they were wondering.

We reassure them that he was sick and they manage to bring him around. They told us they were taking him to the University Hospital, not the Misericordia, which was a five-minute drive from our house. They spent a lot of time with him in the ambulance before leaving with their lightbar flashing.

The doctors in emergency looked him over, he was now on oxygen and they moved him into a more private cubicle. Soon afterwards, they moved him to a glassed-off room and everybody was masking up, putting cloth slippers on their shoes and changing gowns, going in and out of the room. Chris had been to a medi-center earlier. The doctor there thought he had viral meningitis, recommended plenty of fluids and bedrest and thought he'd be better in a week to ten days.

Now the doctors came out of the room, removing their gowns, gloves, masks and shoe-covers and approached us. They thought he had SARS, they were admitting him to the ICU and placing him in quarantine. SARS is a severe and acute respiratory disease that is very infectious and deadly. It had broken out in Ontario that year and several people had died. The next day, someone on the medical team let it slip that they didn't have the proper equipment to protect the staff and others from it.

They gowned us up and let us see our son for a very brief moment. We reassured him as best we could. The hospital staff told us it would be quite a while before he would be installed in the ICU and that we should go home. I suggested to Janet that she leave and get some rest and that I would stay with him tonight and she could stay with him tomorrow during the day. I reassured Chris once again that everything would be fine and that I was staying in the hospital. I wouldn't see him for a while but for him to remember that I was here.

It was a terrible night. I felt completely helpless to do anything for him. While I was never allowed to be in the room with him, I could see him through a small window. He was on oxygen and there were IV's and tubes coming out of his body with beeping monitors besides him. No one went in or out of the room. I could talk to him through an intercom only. While I could see him, I wasn't sure if he could see me.

Janet arrived at eight in the morning. She was frantic and I let her know he was okay so far. I left her there and went to work. At this time, Janet was an admin assistant for a consortium that put on professional development courses for Alberta teachers. She worked across the street from the hospital in the University's Education Building. She mostly sat with Chris all day although she did make a few visits across the road to her office.

We found out later that day that Chris didn't have SARS. The bad news was that he had a very common pneumonia bacterium. Instead of lodging inside his lungs, it had first attacked the outer lining of his lungs, ergo his back pain and sudden fever and the diagnosis of viral meningitis. Then it attacked his heart and his kidneys. They told us that if he was not as young as he was, he would have been placed in an iron lung, something that today sounds bizarre.

Chris was in the ICU for a week. Janet stayed with him in the daytime and his sister Jackie visited after school and I stayed with him during the nights, sleeping on a cot in his room, (he was out of quarantine.) Then he was transferred to a regular ward for a few days and then able to come home.

My bond with Chris strengthened during those nights at his bedside. In the beginning, he wasn't conscious for most of the time; his lung and kidney functions were only at thirty percent when he was admitted so his body shut down anything that wasn't vital.

In the quiet of his isolation room, I took the opportunity to talk to him as I was sure he could still hear me even if it was on an unconscious level. My words reminded him of the contribution he still had to make to the world, in whatever form that may be. At the time he was making comedic films and writing funny scripts so I seized on that. The world needs humour and his place in the scheme of things was to provide it. As well, being born big and strong, he could use this to help others and to make the world a better place.

After recovering Chris decided not to cut his hair, hence the long beard and long hair, the Samson thing that drew women to him like iron to a magnet.

Chris has created his own business, which he has named Ragnar the Trader. He makes and sells what he calls Barbarian Goods. I admire his crafting skills and the way he makes the merchandise he sells. His hand stitching of leather goods looks like it was done on a machine and he has incredibly stable hands that allow him to carve intricate designs on animal horn.

When I see him working at his trade shows, talking and laughing with his customers, I'm proud of him. He is making a difference in this world.

Our daughter Jackie came along a few years after Chris. I was freelancing at the time, shooting documentaries, commercials and corporate videos. It so happened that just around the time she was to be born, I was scheduled on a shoot. I had set up with the producer that he could call on a cameraman friend of mine who would cover for me in the event that she decided to put in her appearance during our three days of shooting. Sure enough, she did.

When I rose that morning, Janet was already awake. This is extremely unusual; her natural rhythm is to get up around ten in the morning and go to bed around two at night. I had taken on the responsibility early in our relationship to wake her every day with lots of time for her to get ready for work and get there on time.

She informed me that her labour had started. I was in panic mode, trying to get dressed and call my friend to cover for me and run into town to give him the gear. Janet handed me a mug of coffee as I headed out the door and our neighbour Carol came in with her son, about Chris' age. What was she doing here? Oh yeah, the plan was that Carol would come over and stay with Janet so that she could take her to the hospital in the event that I didn't make it back in time. I am not one to speed but I may have driven out of character that morning.

I made it back to the acreage and I was relieved to see Janet and Carol chatting away, the boys playing with Chris' wooden train set. I sat down and joined the ladies. Janet gave me a second cup of coffee. Carol and I were deep in conversation and I hadn't even noticed that Janet left the room. She came back in and announced that her water had broken. We rushed around, bundling the boys up in their snowsuits. Carol would watch Chris until I came back from our small local hospital in Stony Plain, Alberta.

Jackie was born a little past noon, we barely got to the hospital in time. After all the hoopla was over, the staff asked us if it would be okay if they went for lunch before moving Janet to another room. They offered to have some food sent in for us.

"I can't believe they are giving us spaghetti and meatballs to eat here in the delivery room!" I said when lunch arrived. Mottled blood still covered the floor. A part of the placenta was hanging out of a waste receptacle. The last thing my wife and I wanted to do was eat, especially slippery, stringy pasta and lumpy meatballs in a red sauce. Janet was still groggy from the delivery, she had lost a lot of blood. What I wanted was my daughter. She had been hustled away to another room and I just wanted to be with her.

We were hoping for a girl since we already had a boy. When it came time to plan a family, we had decided on a small one. Our wish had been granted with this little bundle of girl. We named her Jacqueline Susan. Her middle name is in honour of Janet's twin sister. We had battled over the first name for months before one of us suggested Jackie. We both knew a girl by that name at Humber College and she was a sweet person so it seemed fitting to name our little girl Jackie.

Being born in a small hospital, Jackie was the only baby birthed that day and she received a huge amount of attention from the nurses. They would bring her to Janet wearing the cutest little knitted outfits and wrapped in warm hand-crocheted blankets.

Maybe it was all the times that as a family, we would go for hikes in Edmonton's river valley that gave her an appreciation of nature. The four of us would pack a picnic lunch and spend an afternoon exploring the creeks and ravines, dead branches carved into walking sticks, pretending we were serious explorers.

This strong young woman has certainly taken to the outdoors. They say your kids will do whatever you have done except do it bigger and better. And that is true of Jackie. Every weekend that she can, she heads to the mountains near Jasper, Nordegg or Banff to mountain climb (or ice climb in the winter.) We both enjoy cycling in the mountains and that love has led us to bikepack the Kettle Valley Railway together.

Once on one of our trips, I saw that the picnic table was in flames. Unnoticed by me, the camp fuel I had been pouring into my stove had overflowed onto the table top. I had not been paying much attention while speaking to a German tourist at the same time as lighting my stove for lunch. The man wanted to know the history of the railway bridge behind us. I flicked my lighter and the table erupted into flames, the inquiring fellow backed away with a worried look on his face. Maybe he thought he was to be sacrificed in some sort of backwoods ritual.

Thinking quickly, I managed to smother the flames with a space blanket. I looked over at my daughter who was rolling her eyes. It was only lunchtime on the first day of a multiple day bikepacking trip and things were not going exactly to plan.

Jackie and I had completed the MS Mountain Tour as a warm-up to this trip. While described as an entry level mountain biking experience, I found the two forty-five-kilometer days to be grueling. Jackie, a strong and physically fit young woman, seemed to breeze along. At the banquet after the first day, she danced late into the night while I had to go to bed after one beer. She loves the mountains and spending two days riding a bike on its forested slopes and raising money for a good cause was heaven for her.

Usually at Christmastime, Jackie is the one who records each gift as it is opened, who received it and who it's from. One year, when she was five, she looked up from the notebook and saw that there was a small present wrapped in purple-blue paper under the tree. Lying there, all by itself, dried up pine needles sprinkled on its top where they had fallen from the tree. Unopened, just like on other Christmases.

"Daddy, Daddy, can I open it this year?" she asks.

"I'm afraid you can't Jackie. I vowed never to open it a long time ago."

"But I don't understand. It is a present and it is for you." She is perplexed.

"It's a long story and I won't ever open it."

She thought about this for a while and with a bright smile she asked, "can I open it when you are dead?"

That last question of hers hangs in the air. My wife, her patience worn out with the ever-present gift, has come to a decision.

"Michael, (what she calls me when she is being firm,) I don't want you to put that present under the tree again. You can see how it upsets the children and they are too young to understand your reasons for keeping it. Put it back wherever it is that you keep it. If you want to pull it out and look at it every Christmas, do it away from us!"

Jackie has grown into a fine young woman, very confident and wise. She has an ability to see into the characters of others, she is a very sharp negotiator. With her winning smile, she can easily put people at ease and she has a ton of friends and acquaintances.

She is the only one in our household that has taken up my peculiar habit of toasting the Donnelly's every February fourth with a shot of whiskey.

"Here's to us!"

"Who's like us?"

"Devil a one!"

"And they're all dead!"

It was on February fourth, 1880 that the Donnelly's of Lucan, Ontario were massacred by a vigilante group composed of neighbours and local townspeople. My interest in the Donnelly's began in the early '70's when I read Thomas P. Kelly's sensational books about the Canadian tragedy. The Donnelly story makes the Hatfield-McCoy feud seem like a sandbox fight. My interest was ignited when I was a chef at the Seven Dwarfs restaurant in London, Ontario. One of the other chefs, Danny, an Irishman himself, told me his family once owned the Donnelly homestead and he interested me with tales of vandalism and harassment at the farm.

My brother-in-law Paul knew of the place and took me to the Catholic cemetery where they were buried. Armed with an 8mm film camera, I documented the excrement on the tombstone and the broken beer bottles on their graves. It appeared then that the feud still lived on after ninety-three years.

In 1979, living and working in Edmonton, it occurred to me that the 100th anniversary of the massacre was only months away. Going there would require stepping out of my comfort zone, but I decided that I just had to be there that night. Uninvited. I need not have worried. With my twin lens reflex camera around my neck, I could pass myself off as a pro. Perhaps it was the distance I had travelled to be there. I was greeted warmly and invited to join the others around the kitchen table where already a group of hard-core enthusiasts sat swapping stories. A descendant of one of the killers and a descendant of the only witness to the crime were amongst the group.

Mostly what I remember of the night is what I recorded with my camera: Ontario Provincial Police officers directing traffic and preventing the crowds from entering the homestead, a fire set by vandals, artifacts dug up from the property, and a group toasting the Donnelly's over the site of the original farmhouse exactly to the minute of the massacre a hundred years previously.

Over the years, Jackie has caught 'Donnelly Fever' from listening to my tales. Our joint interest has us competing every year to see who can greet the other first on this day with "Happy Donnelly Day!" Then I enjoy my toast with my daughter, who otherwise is pretty much a non-drinker.

As I write, I look over at Jackie in her office across the basement from mine. I feel a strong sense of pride at what an incredible person she has become. Running a successful business, one that helps people, she works very hard. I admire her organizational skills which I think she inherited from her maternal grandmother; a woman who, having raised a family of seven children, knew all about organization.

I see my own mother in her too. In her retirement, my mother had taken up French cooking using my hardcover cookbook from cooking school. While Jackie, at sixteen, was on a trip to Ontario that she organized by herself, she asked my mother to teach her some of her recipes. Jackie's specialty is Granny's rum balls. They are so strong you have to keep them away from open flame.

One of my favourite photos of Jackie shows her in the kitchen, wearing a cute red dress, mixing bowl tucked under her tiny arm, stirring batter with a wooden spoon, a joyful look on her face. She was three. All of her friends know of the frequent meals she prepares. As part of her teaching others about energy, she makes lunches and snacks for her students with very carefully prepared dishes that complement the energy work they are conducting. She often invites one of more of her friends to come to the house for a meal and they always exclaim over her culinary delights.

This past Thanksgiving (the first weekend in October in Canada,) it was cold and blustery. There were roofers frantically trying to finish up their job in the row of houses behind our home. Snow was in the overnight forecast. We had taken a rest from our feast before dessert and had started a board game. Jackie had made a maple pecan pie. She asked us how much pie we'd each like. After cutting our portions, she went to the door, donned her coat and shoes and took the rest of the pie to the roofers. She said their smiles were as big as the moon. I was so proud of my beautiful, thoughtful and generous daughter.

All that said, my daughter is vegan and it is very unlikely that she will ever serve spaghetti and meatballs. Meatballs made out of meat that is.

14 My Gut Speaks

After Chris was born, Janet did not want to return to work, she could not abide the idea of someone else raising our baby. I agreed with her. However, we soon missed her income. At work, I was once again faced with breaking in a new reporter. I decided the time was right to go freelance. Through Janet's work, I had made a lot of valuable contacts and they were encouraging me to go on my own. That way they could hire me.

Spending sixty thousand dollars for the camera, let alone the other equipment like a tripod, a lighting kit and microphones was a bit nerve-wracking. I soon had a steady stream of clients and their projects to work on and I brought in more money than the two of us combined had earned.

Unfortunately, six years later, we were in a recession and there were huge cut-backs that especially affected my bottom line. You could now buy a camera for half of what I had paid and more cameramen who had been laid off were doing just that. I cut my prices then reached a point of no returns. It was time to find something else to do. I had one last shoot booked and a buyer on the hook for my production company.

I was contracted by a company from Ontario. Once we agreed on the price, (not cut-rate), their instructions were clear and simple. I was to go to a certain room at the convention center and set up my camera, tripod, lights and a lavalier microphone. People would come into the room and I was to hook up the microphone and record whatever they said. Pretty simple.

After a while, a stream of well-dressed and well-groomed men and women came into the room and I recorded them. They all spoke of making lots of money and having lots of fun.

That evening, while the kids were in bed, I rewound the tapes and played them back for Janet to see what she thought of them. We had never heard of NSA and with my production company hurting, we needed to look for a new way to make money. One of the people had given me his card and I called him. He invited me to a meeting in a few days.

I sat attentively through the demonstration of the products which were water and air filtration units for home use. The room was full. The last half of the meeting involved some of the same people I had filmed. They talked again about how much money they were making and how easy it was. Hmmm. Dennis, the man who had invited me, wanted to know if I wanted to sign up and join in selling these products. I told him I'd have to think about it. I wasn't one hundred percent convinced.

At the next meeting, it was the same formula. A demonstration of the products and then some people got up and said the same thing I had heard before, now for the third time. "What's going on here?" I think. "Haven't these people made any new money since I first filmed them?" An alarm bell began going off in my gut. Something wasn't right here.

Why does anyone do an irrational thing? I can't explain why I signed up. I can't tell you why I took the proceeds from the sale of my production company and bought a huge amount of these products. Now my job was to call my friends and associates and get them to buy these items and to get them to join NSA.

Most of the people I called were gracious in declining my offer and some of them had quite a lot to say about multi-level marketing. Which is what this was.

I did make a few sales because these were excellent products. However, I had not made enough sales to make ends meet. We always made sure the kids were well fed, even if that meant that some nights we had popcorn for supper after they were in bed. We didn't want them asking us awkward questions about our meal.

In my desperation, I stumbled across an idea as to how to sell this stuff. It involved setting up an air and water filter into a business and letting them try the products for free for a week. I chose in particular, smelly places like auto body repair shops, denture labs and nail salons.

What surprised me was that I began to sell the products that I had placed. Cash started to flow in and my large inventory began to dwindle. I started to think that perhaps I had some sales skills. If it were true, I came by it naturally, I thought, as my maternal grandfather was a successful salesman in Wales, selling coal of all things.

One of my associates bragged about her brother; how he had been a meat cutter in a packing plant and now made a lot of money selling cemetery plots. The same kind of money I had made freelancing. My stock of air filters and water filters was getting low and I was reluctant to order more. I wanted out of NSA.

Scanning the want ads in The Journal, I saw a job advertised that was looking for salespeople for a cemetery. Could this be the same deal that the lady had talked about? I made an appointment. The man who interviewed me told me that if I did what he told me to do, I could make one hundred thousand dollars in my first year. Sounded interesting but I was skeptical. I had been burned before and really, not so long ago either.

I called up the ex-meat cutter and described what the sales manager had told me and that I didn't believe him. "Well, he's the same guy who trained me and if you do what he says, you'll make that kind of money!" he told me. That is how I became a cemetery plot salesman. And yes, I have heard all the jokes about that profession. "Must be a dead-end job. People are dying to buy from you, etc., etc."

I also learned one of the most valuable lessons of my life: LISTEN TO YOUR GUT. If I had listened to those alarm bells ringing in my gut then I never would have gotten involved in NSA. It has saved my butt many times since.

The children were attending school and we had moved to a rental property in the city. Janet picked up all the slack at home as I was working twelve to fourteen-hour days. I was earning good coin; however, it was feast and famine. Janet had learnt many economical tips from her mom and we coasted along as best we could. Eventually, we bought a home in the city, the one we live in today.

Once Chris and Jackie were both in junior high, Janet went back to work. BC (before children,) she had worked as a sound recordist and mixer and everything was analog. Now, everything was digital. Her skills were just about obsolete. She decided to find an office job. This led her to return to school, enrolled in a nine-month fast-tracked IT course, sponsored by our provincial telecommunications corporation. They wanted trained people for their internet help desk and had created the course with a local community college. They were promising to start people at the lofty sum of twenty-two dollars an hour and offered part time work, about thirty hours per week. It sounded ideal. I was now an assistant manager at the cemetery and with the crazy hours I was putting in, Janet working part time would be perfect for our family.

Then came a catch. Halfway through the course, the company merged with a similar corporation in British Columbia. They instilled a hiring freeze. No one was hired for the help desk. Ever the trouper, Janet found a full time receptionist job that paid twelve dollars an hour. With super fantastic computer skills and her smarts, about every two years she changed jobs, always moving to a better position; she was now working as an office assistant and beginning to earn a decent salary.

This was around my forty-seventh birthday. I was a mess that day. My father was forty-seven when he died of a massive heart attack and I thought I was to meet a similar fate. I kept tapping myself all over, checking to see if I was really there. Finally, Janet asked me what was going on. I levelled with her.

I told her I was unhappy. I did not feel fulfilled. I did not feel I was doing the work I should be doing. I hated my job. I was missing a lot of what was happening with the kids. I wanted a change. She asked me what I wanted to do and I told her I wanted to work in television again. Always my supporter, she said, "go for it."

I applied for a job at A-Channel as a technical director where they told me my skills were out of date. They offered me a weekend job operating their 'Live' truck at not much more than minimum wage. Dejected, I came home and told Janet. She said, "go for it." She felt she was making enough money to keep us going as long as we watched our pennies and cut back a bit and she felt it was her chance to step up to the plate and take some of the financial pressure off of me.

I was still selling Monday to Friday so the station's lousy pay would be acceptable. When I was interviewed, they asked me why someone with my resume would want to work there? I told the news director that I was a gambler. I was willing to gamble on myself; that a better paying position would open up and I would be qualified to get that job.

Within three months a job did open up in the Creative Department as an Electronic Field Production (EFP) camera operator. The Creative Director poached me into his department. I wasn't making nearly as much money as I had made as a salesman, yet between the two of us, working full time, we were making ends meet. More important, we were both happy.

A few years passed, the kids had graduated from high school, life looked good. We had helped our son and his wife buy a small house in Yorkton,

Saskatchewan and Christmas was approaching. They did not have a car and often complained of the long walk to and from the grocery store. Janet wanted to buy them a mid-sized freezer for Christmas to make things easier for them.

We were shopping at Sears. I wasn't feeling well and kept throwing myself onto the top of various appliances. My chest was heavy, I was trying to get my muscles to relax. I tried leaning against a refrigerator; it didn't help matters. The handle dug deeply into my kidneys. Next, I tried squatting down on my haunches, a position I had copied from my scout leader when I was a kid and have found it to be very comfortable. Janet had engaged with a salesman who was showing her various models of smaller freezers.

Staying in my squat, I got really hot, I stood for a moment and took off my jacket, then threw myself over a washing machine. Suddenly I got really cold and put my jacket back on. Janet and the salesman were proceeding with the sale without me. She kept giving me looks, wondering what I was up to.

I went back to my squat, now I could feel a sharp pain travelling down the length of my left arm. It felt like an electric shock. Oh no! Could this be? The answer came quickly as the pain raced up my left arm. OMG! A heart attack? And the negotiations were still ongoing over my head.

I stood up and told Janet we had to leave, right away. She looked at me and defiantly asked, "why?"

"Because I think I am having a heart attack," I answered.

"We'll call an ambulance," said the salesman.

"No," I said, grabbing Janet's arm, "you can drive me."

Having been a salesman, I ruefully thought that when the young man who was helping Janet went for his lunch, he probably took a lot of ribbing over his lost sale and the unique objection I had crafted. He probably defended himself with something like:

"Come on! The guy was totally believable! The way the guy kept squirming around and distracting his wife. She told me to just ignore him." And his co-workers probably laughed at him and replied with something rude like: "he probably just needed to have a crap!"

I not only made my frantic wife drive me to the hospital, I refused to go to the nearest one and insisted she drive me to the University Hospital, a further twenty minutes away. At one point, I leaned over her and honked the horn at the car in front of us to get the guy to make a left-hand turn and not sit there all day. Janet turned and looked at me. She calmly said, "you can no longer ever say anything about my back-seat driving."

When we got to the hospital, Janet signaled to pull into emergency.

"Don't do that," I said, now feeling a bit better. "Go park across the street at the Education Building, it'll be a lot cheaper."

She gave me a hard look then followed my orders. After parking, as we crossed the street on foot, my pain came back and I doubled over. Janet gave me supreme shit and helped me to the sidewalk. Once we were in the hospital, I insisted on stopping to go to the washroom. I think at this point, Janet almost lost it but she gave in. Maye she was thinking what's the difference if I kill him or he dies of a heart attack alone, in a hospital washroom?

Once we made it to the emergency department, we were shocked to find it empty. There was not one person waiting in the whole place, this on a Saturday morning in early winter. They asked me what the problem was and I said I was having a heart attack. Three sets of hands grabbed me and I knew I'd be well cared for, while Janet, white-faced, sat alone in the empty waiting room.

A cluster of wires extends from my chest to a wheeled stand full of beeping, buzzing and flashing medical equipment. This is the fourth day of lying on my back, the longest period of time I have ever spent in bed. But then I'd never had a heart attack before.

My family and good friends have all left to go about their daily lives and I am here alone in my room on the cardiac floor of our local hospital. Bored to tears. Hungry as hell too. The portions of food given to heart attack patients wouldn't sustain a bird. My stomach is shrinking and if this continues much longer, I fear that I will disappear.

A book reader would think that this is a fantastic opportunity to read but right now I am all read out. Janet has kindly brought me some books from home and I had to put down "The Hungry Cyclist." His descriptions of the meals he samples across the Americas causes my stomach to rumble, my mouth to salivate. I want to ring the nurses and beg for food but I know it is useless; they will refuse my pleas.

Breakfast consisted of a lonely piece of dry toast, and a tiny cup of fruit salad. No coffee for this boy! Lunch had been not much better; a green salad and a bowl of broth. Looking around, I notice that I had placed the book on top of this evening's supper menu. In my emaciated state, I grab it almost afraid of what it may say.

A hamburger with all the fixings! Oh boy! This is going to be good. And it has all the fixin's. All afternoon I lie there, images of translucent fried onions smother the top. Pickles hide under the onions. A thick slab of bright orange cheddar cheese melts down the sides of a patty that must be two inches thick. Sprinkled over the toasted bun are sesame seeds, artfully scattered. I was really getting into this daydream. It reminded me of how Second World War Allied prisoners would, instead of a bedtime story, or moon about missing loved ones, take turns describing the first meal they would eat when the war ended.

My stomach growled in anticipation. My mouth watered uncontrollably. Why not fantasize? There was nothing else to do. I eagerly awaited supper and when it was brought in to me, I couldn't wait to rip off the shiny metal cover and dig in.

I nearly cried. Seriously. The burger with all the fixin's was no bigger than a slider. The patty was a thin institutional piece of meat product. Dejectedly lifting the naked bun top, I could see there was no cheese. A slight smear of mustard and a scrawny piece of iceberg lettuce was the hospital's idea of 'all the fixings.' When was I going to learn that my diet would need to change? Meagre portions like this were my new reality.

Recovering from a heart attack is a strange experience. It wasn't mandatory, but Janet and I enrolled in Heart Attack School at the city's rehabilitation hospital. It had a more clinical name like "Post-Operative Cardiac Awareness Training" or something in that vein. The first class was a communal gathering in the hospital's auditorium and the first thing we were told was that our new reality involved vigorous exercise for the rest of our lives.

This was followed by a very loud collective groan from the crowd of about one hundred men. The guy seated next to me complained out loud, "you didn't say this was going to be so hard!"

I felt a bit smug. I had always been a great walker and most of the year, I rode my bicycle to work, about fifteen kilometers each way. I have a weight bench in the basement and use it regularly. Today, whenever I'm in the gym, I think about all my heart school classmates and I wonder if they are still exercising vigorously every day. I know I try my best. No way I'm going back there.

I am so much more in tune with my feelings than at any other time in my life. I had a younger boss whose father had recently suffered a heart attack, and he was more than generous with time off and in slowly easing me back to my full workload. I felt very grateful to him.

A year or so later, at my physical, I asked my doctor about a brown spot on my right arm that my wife insisted I get looked at. "Keep your eye on it. If it changes, colour, shape or texture, let me know," said our family doctor. The thing was, that as soon as I started watching it, it did change, shape, colour and texture. As though my thoughts were controlling it.

A week later, the doctor took a tiny slice out of my arm and stitched me up. I had an appointment the next week to have the stitches taken out. By then he would have the biopsy results.

Two days later, I'm on a shoot at a local high school when my cellphone rings. The display shows that it is the doctor's office calling. A nurse on the other end of the line tells me, "Mr. Pearce, we have you scheduled for surgery this afternoon at two o'clock."

"What are you talking about? Surgery? What on earth for? I can't go for surgery! I'm on a shoot!"

"That's fine Mr. Pearce. You're going to see the doctor soon to have the stitches taken out and he can talk to you then," she says.

I involve myself in setting up lights in a gymnasium and then my phone rings. The doctor's office again. What do they want now?

This time it is our family doctor calling. In the twenty-five years he has been our family doctor, I have never spoken to him on the phone. This was unusual. "We have you scheduled for surgery, Adrian," He starts off.

"What do I need surgery for?" I ask. I'm getting impatient. Our shoot starts soon and I have much work to do.

"You have the worst skin cancer you can get," he tells me.

I nearly faint.

"But we have you scheduled with an excellent surgeon. He is very excited to see you and he can cure you. He can't cure most of the people he treats."

I thank the doctor and agree to be there at two o'clock. I then call Janet with the news. My voice quakes as I tell her. Always the steadfast partner, she calms me and reminds me that I can be cured that day. Cured from the Big C.

My producer Gord almost drops to the ground when I tell him my news. Gord is a very understanding man. He told me to drop everything and to go. He would figure out this shoot. My health was the most important thing.

I take my station vehicle back downtown. My boss, having previously dealt with my heart attack, knew what to do. He finagled another cameraman for the shoot and I was free to go. I jumped on my bike and rode way down to the south side of the city about fifteen kilometers away.

Almost immediately, I was ushered into a surgical room where I sat on an examination table still wearing my bike shirt, shorts, bike shoes and gloves. My helmet rested beside me. When the doctor entered the room the first thing he said to me was, "you're not planning to ride home are you?"

"Yes sir. It's a short ride back to my place," I answer.

"No way. You are having surgery and I want you to call someone to come and pick you up."

Maybe this is more serious than I thought. More than just a biopsy. I call Janet, my voice even shakier and Janet agrees to pick me up and she'll bring Jackie who can help load my bike into the car.

In the process of the surgery, he took out a piece of my forearm about the size of a toonie and right down to the muscle. I was conscious the whole time although they wouldn't let me watch. I figured they didn't want me puking into an open wound. The whole procedure took an hour and I was 'cured.' I knew I was cured by the relieved comments the doctor made when he discovered there were no tendrils (his word) going into the muscle.

I called Janet and waited for her outside. We went to the pharmacy in the same building to buy special dressings to use at home to keep the wound wrapped. The nurses had given me a demonstration on how to wrap the surgical site.

My loving wife and daughter got me home and installed in my Lazy Boy and I rested the better part of that day, with my bike stowed in the garage. I was in shock since it all had happened so suddenly.

One day I'm a healthy man and the next I am a cancer victim.

The next day I felt a little better and decided to join Janet and Jackie on a garage sale expedition. Big mistake. My emotions were so fragile that after two stops, I insisted they take me home. I could not handle the sensory input of something as simple as going to garage sales.

At the second garage sale, I scored a stereo system for twenty bucks. Now I could connect our turntable to the amplifier and speakers I had just bought. It was a simple matter to hook it all up and I could listen to my favourite vinyl, in my Lazy Boy, which comforted me.

My buddy Roy was understanding when I told him that we would have to postpone our bikepacking adventure until I healed. So much of my arm had been removed that there was still an open wound that would not close up. Having been bikepacking in the wilds before, I knew that it usually is a less than hygienic environment and I didn't want to have to deal with an infection on top of everything else.

Roy and I did make the trip after the wound had closed enough to be covered simply with a bandage. When I look at photos of that trip, I can see visible changes in myself over the course of the week we spent in the woods. A photo taken at the beginning of the trip shows me looking diminished. My helmet is askew and I am hunched over the handlebars of my bike. Yet in a photo Roy took of me five and a half days later in the Myra Canyon, I look engaged. My camping gear is stacked neatly on my bike and my helmet is fitting properly. My legs are firm. I look as I always look on these trips I make with Roy. Healthy. Strong.

It never surprises me how quickly the body will adapt to physical exertion. The very bikepacking trip that I was nervous about taking is one of the very things that helped to heal me. My recovery was shortened by the love and support of my family. Just like when we went through hard times and had lost everything, we discovered we had all we needed: LoveAfter Chris was born, Janet did not want to return to work, she could not abide the idea of someone else raising our baby. I agreed with her. However, we soon missed her income. At work, I was once again faced with breaking in a new reporter. I decided the time was right to go freelance. Through Janet's work, I had made a lot of valuable contacts and they were encouraging me to go on my own. That way they could hire me.

Spending sixty thousand dollars for the camera, let alone the other equipment like a tripod, a lighting kit and microphones was a bit nerve-wracking. I soon had a steady stream of clients and their projects to work on and I brought in more money than the two of us combined had earned.

Unfortunately, six years later, we were in a recession and there were huge cut-backs that especially affected my bottom line. You could now buy a camera for half of what I had paid and more cameramen who had been laid off were doing just that. I cut my prices then reached a point of no returns. It was time to find something else to do. I had one last shoot booked and a buyer on the hook for my production company.

I was contracted by a company from Ontario. Once we agreed on the price, (not cut-rate), their instructions were clear and simple. I was to go to a certain room at the convention center and set up my camera, tripod, lights and a lavalier microphone.

People would come into the room and I was to hook up the microphone and record whatever they said. Pretty simple.

After a while, a stream of well-dressed and well-groomed men and women came into the room and I recorded them. They all spoke of making lots of money and having lots of fun.

That evening, while the kids were in bed, I rewound the tapes and played them back for Janet to see what she thought of them. We had never heard of NSA and with my production company hurting, we needed to look for a new way to make money. One of the people had given me his card and I called him. He invited me to a meeting in a few days.

I sat attentively through the demonstration of the products which were water and air filtration units for home use. The room was full. The last half of the meeting involved some of the same people I had filmed. They talked again about how much money they were making and how easy it was. Hmmm. Dennis, the man who had invited me, wanted to know if I wanted to sign up and join in selling these products. I told him I'd have to think about it. I wasn't one hundred percent convinced.

At the next meeting, it was the same formula. A demonstration of the products and then some people got up and said the same thing I had heard before, now for the third time. "What's going on here?" I think. "Haven't these people made any new money since I first filmed them?" An alarm bell began going off in my gut. Something wasn't right here.

Why does anyone do an irrational thing? I can't explain why I signed up. I can't tell you why I took the proceeds from the sale of my production company and bought a huge amount of these products. Now my job was to call my friends and associates and get them to buy these items and to get them to join NSA.

Most of the people I called were gracious in declining my offer and some of them had quite a lot to say about multi-level marketing. Which is what this was.

I did make a few sales because these were excellent products. However, I had not made enough sales to make ends meet. We always made sure the kids were well fed, even if that meant that some nights we had popcorn for supper after they were in bed. We didn't want them asking us awkward questions about our meal.

In my desperation, I stumbled across an idea as to how to sell this stuff. It involved setting up an air and water filter into a business and letting them try the products for free for a week. I chose in particular, smelly places like auto body repair shops, denture labs and nail salons.

What surprised me was that I began to sell the products that I had placed. Cash started to flow in and my large inventory began to dwindle. I started to think that perhaps I had some sales skills. If it were true, I came by it naturally, I thought, as my maternal grandfather was a successful salesman in Wales, selling coal of all things.

One of my associates bragged about her brother; how he had been a meat cutter in a packing plant and now made a lot of money selling cemetery plots. The same kind of money I had made freelancing. My stock of air filters and water filters was getting low and I was reluctant to order more. I wanted out of NSA.

Scanning the want ads in The Journal, I saw a job advertised that was looking for salespeople for a cemetery. Could this be the same deal that the lady had talked about? I made an appointment. The man who interviewed me told me that if I did what he told me to do, I could make one hundred thousand dollars in my first year. Sounded interesting but I was skeptical. I had been burned before and really, not so long ago either.

I called up the ex-meat cutter and described what the sales manager had told me and that I didn't believe him. "Well, he's the same guy who trained me and if you do what he says, you'll make that kind of money!" he told me. That is how I became a cemetery plot salesman. And yes, I have heard all the jokes about that profession. "Must be a dead-end job. People are dying to buy from you, etc., etc."

I also learned one of the most valuable lessons of my life: LISTEN TO YOUR GUT. If I had listened to those alarm bells ringing in my gut then I never would have gotten involved in NSA. It has saved my butt many times since.

The children were attending school and we had moved to a rental property in the city. Janet picked up all the slack at home as I was working twelve to fourteen-hour days. I was earning good coin; however, it was feast and famine. Janet had learnt many economical tips from her mom and we coasted along as best we could. Eventually, we bought a home in the city, the one we live in today.

Once Chris and Jackie were both in junior high, Janet went back to work. BC (before children,) she had worked as a sound recordist and mixer and everything was analog. Now, everything was digital. Her skills were just about obsolete. She decided to find an office job. This led her to return to school, enrolled in a nine-month fast-tracked IT course, sponsored by our provincial telecommunications corporation. They wanted trained people for their internet help desk and had created the course with a local community college. They were promising to start people at the lofty sum of twenty-two dollars an hour and offered part time work, about thirty hours per week. It sounded ideal. I was now an assistant manager at the cemetery and with the crazy hours I was putting in, Janet working part time would be perfect for our family.

Then came a catch. Halfway through the course, the company merged with a similar corporation in British Columbia. They instilled a hiring freeze. No one was hired for the help desk. Ever the trouper, Janet found a full time receptionist job that paid twelve dollars an hour. With super fantastic computer skills and her smarts, about every two years she changed jobs, always moving to a better position; she was now working as an office assistant and beginning to earn a decent salary.

This was around my forty-seventh birthday. I was a mess that day. My father was forty-seven when he died of a massive heart attack and I thought I was to meet a similar fate. I kept tapping myself all over, checking to see if I was really there. Finally, Janet asked me what was going on. I levelled with her.

I told her I was unhappy. I did not feel fulfilled. I did not feel I was doing the work I should be doing. I hated my job. I was missing a lot of what was happening with the kids. I wanted a change. She asked me what I wanted to do and I told her I wanted to work in television again. Always my supporter, she said, "go for it."

I applied for a job at A-Channel as a technical director where they told me my skills were out of date. They offered me a weekend job operating their 'Live' truck at not much more than minimum wage.

Dejected, I came home and told Janet. She said, "go for it." She felt she was making enough money to keep us going as long as we watched our pennies and cut back a bit and she felt it was her chance to step up to the plate and take some of the financial pressure off of me.

I was still selling Monday to Friday so the station's lousy pay would be acceptable. When I was interviewed, they asked me why someone with my resume would want to work there? I told the news director that I was a gambler. I was willing to gamble on myself; that a better paying position would open up and I would be qualified to get that job.

Within three months a job did open up in the Creative Department as an Electronic Field Production (EFP) camera operator. The Creative Director poached me into his department. I wasn't making nearly as much money as I had made as a salesman, yet between the two of us, working full time, we were making ends meet. More important, we were both happy.

A few years passed, the kids had graduated from high school, life looked good. We had helped our son and his wife buy a small house in Yorkton, Saskatchewan and Christmas was approaching. They did not have a car and often complained of the long walk to and from the grocery store. Janet wanted to buy them a mid-sized freezer for Christmas to make things easier for them.

We were shopping at Sears. I wasn't feeling well and kept throwing myself onto the top of various appliances. My chest was heavy, I was trying to get my muscles to relax. I tried leaning against a refrigerator; it didn't help matters. The handle dug deeply into my kidneys. Next, I tried squatting down on my haunches, a position I had copied from my scout leader when I was a kid and have found it to be very comfortable. Janet had engaged with a salesman who was showing her various models of smaller freezers.

Staying in my squat, I got really hot, I stood for a moment and took off my jacket, then threw myself over a washing machine. Suddenly I got really cold and put my jacket back on. Janet and the salesman were proceeding with the sale without me. She kept giving me looks, wondering what I was up to.

I went back to my squat, now I could feel a sharp pain travelling down the length of my left arm. It felt like an electric shock. Oh no! Could this be? The answer came quickly as the pain raced up my left arm. OMG! A heart attack? And the negotiations were still ongoing over my head.

I stood up and told Janet we had to leave, right away. She looked at me and defiantly asked, "why?"

"Because I think I am having a heart attack," I answered.

"We'll call an ambulance," said the salesman.

"No," I said, grabbing Janet's arm, "you can drive me."

Having been a salesman, I ruefully thought that when the young man who was helping Janet went for his lunch, he probably took a lot of ribbing over his lost sale and the unique objection I had crafted. He probably defended himself with something like:

"Come on! The guy was totally believable! The way the guy kept squirming around and distracting his wife. She told me to just ignore him." And his co-workers probably laughed at him and replied with something rude like: "he probably just needed to have a crap!"

I not only made my frantic wife drive me to the hospital, I refused to go to the nearest one and insisted she drive me to the University Hospital, a further twenty minutes away. At one point, I leaned over her and honked the horn at the car in front of us to get the guy to make a left-hand turn and not sit there all day. Janet turned and looked at me. She calmly said, "you can no longer ever say anything about my back-seat driving."

When we got to the hospital, Janet signaled to pull into emergency.

"Don't do that," I said, now feeling a bit better. "Go park across the street at the Education Building, it'll be a lot cheaper."

She gave me a hard look then followed my orders. After parking, as we crossed the street on foot, my pain came back and I doubled over. Janet gave me supreme shit and helped me to the sidewalk. Once we were in the hospital, I insisted on stopping to go to the washroom. I think at this point, Janet almost lost it but she gave in. Maye she was thinking what's the difference if I kill him or he dies of a heart attack alone, in a hospital washroom?

Once we made it to the emergency department, we were shocked to find it empty. There was not one person waiting in the whole place, this on a Saturday morning in early winter. They asked me what the problem was and I said I was having a heart attack. Three sets of hands grabbed me and I knew I'd be well cared for, while Janet, white-faced, sat alone in the empty waiting room.

A cluster of wires extends from my chest to a wheeled stand full of beeping, buzzing and flashing medical equipment. This is the fourth day of lying on my back, the longest period of time I have ever spent in bed. But then I'd never had a heart attack before.

My family and good friends have all left to go about their daily lives and I am here alone in my room on the cardiac floor of our local hospital. Bored to tears. Hungry as hell too. The portions of food given to heart attack patients wouldn't sustain a bird. My stomach is shrinking and if this continues much longer, I fear that I will disappear.

A book reader would think that this is a fantastic opportunity to read but right now I am all read out. Janet has kindly brought me some books from home and I had to put down "The Hungry Cyclist." His descriptions of the meals he samples across the Americas causes my stomach to rumble, my mouth to salivate. I want to ring the nurses and beg for food but I know it is useless; they will refuse my pleas.

Breakfast consisted of a lonely piece of dry toast, and a tiny cup of fruit salad. No coffee for this boy! Lunch had been not much better; a green salad and a bowl of broth. Looking around, I notice that I had placed the book on top of this evening's supper menu. In my emaciated state, I grab it almost afraid of what it may say.

A hamburger with all the fixings! Oh boy! This is going to be good. And it has all the fixin's. All afternoon I lie there, images of translucent fried onions smother the top. Pickles hide under the onions. A thick slab of bright orange cheddar cheese melts down the sides of a patty that must be two inches thick. Sprinkled over the toasted bun are sesame seeds, artfully scattered. I was really getting into this daydream. It reminded me of how Second World War Allied prisoners would, instead of a bedtime story, or moon about missing loved ones, take turns describing the first meal they would eat when the war ended.

My stomach growled in anticipation. My mouth watered uncontrollably. Why not fantasize? There was nothing else to do. I eagerly awaited supper and when it was brought in to me, I couldn't wait to rip off the shiny metal cover and dig in.

I nearly cried. Seriously. The burger with all the fixin's was no bigger than a slider. The patty was a thin institutional piece of meat product. Dejectedly lifting the naked bun top, I could see there was no cheese. A slight smear of mustard and a scrawny piece of iceberg lettuce was the hospital's idea of 'all the fixings.' When was I going to learn that my diet would need to change? Meagre portions like this were my new reality.

Recovering from a heart attack is a strange experience. It wasn't mandatory, but Janet and I enrolled in Heart Attack School at the city's rehabilitation hospital. It had a more clinical name like "Post-Operative Cardiac Awareness Training" or something in that vein. The first class was a communal gathering in the hospital's auditorium and the first thing we were told was that our new reality involved vigorous exercise for the rest of our lives. This was followed by a very loud collective groan from the crowd of about one hundred men. The guy seated next to me complained out loud, "you didn't say this was going to be so hard!"

I felt a bit smug. I had always been a great walker and most of the year, I rode my bicycle to work, about fifteen kilometers each way. I have a weight bench in the basement and use it regularly. Today, whenever I'm in the gym, I think about all my heart school classmates and I wonder if they are still exercising vigorously every day. I know I try my best. No way I'm going back there.

I am so much more in tune with my feelings than at any other time in my life. I had a younger boss whose father had recently suffered a heart attack, and he was more than generous with time off and in slowly easing me back to my full workload. I felt very grateful to him.

A year or so later, at my physical, I asked my doctor about a brown spot on my right arm that my wife insisted I get looked at. "Keep your eye on it. If it changes, colour, shape or texture, let me know," said our family doctor. The thing was, that as soon as I started watching it, it did change, shape, colour and texture. As though my thoughts were controlling it.

A week later, the doctor took a tiny slice out of my arm and stitched me up. I had an appointment the next week to have the stitches taken out. By then he would have the biopsy results.

Two days later, I'm on a shoot at a local high school when my cellphone rings. The display shows that it is the doctor's office calling. A nurse on the other end of the line tells me, "Mr. Pearce, we have you scheduled for surgery this afternoon at two o'clock."

"What are you talking about? Surgery? What on earth for? I can't go for surgery! I'm on a shoot!"

"That's fine Mr. Pearce. You're going to see the doctor soon to have the stitches taken out and he can talk to you then," she says.

I involve myself in setting up lights in a gymnasium and then my phone rings. The doctor's office again. What do they want now?

This time it is our family doctor calling. In the twenty-five years he has been our family doctor, I have never spoken to him on the phone. This was unusual. "We have you scheduled for surgery, Adrian," He starts off.

"What do I need surgery for?" I ask. I'm getting impatient. Our shoot starts soon and I have much work to do.

"You have the worst skin cancer you can get," he tells me.

I nearly faint.

"But we have you scheduled with an excellent surgeon. He is very excited to see you and he can cure you. He can't cure most of the people he treats."

I thank the doctor and agree to be there at two o'clock. I then call Janet with the news. My voice quakes as I tell her. Always the steadfast partner, she calms me and reminds me that I can be cured that day. Cured from the Big C.

My producer Gord almost drops to the ground when I tell him my news. Gord is a very understanding man. He told me to drop everything and to go. He would figure out this shoot. My health was the most important thing.

I take my station vehicle back downtown. My boss, having previously dealt with my heart attack, knew what to do. He finagled another cameraman for the shoot and I was free to go. I jumped on my bike and rode way down to the south side of the city about fifteen kilometers away.

Almost immediately, I was ushered into a surgical room where I sat on an examination table still wearing my bike shirt, shorts, bike shoes and gloves. My helmet rested beside me. When the doctor entered the room the first thing he said to me was, "you're not planning to ride home are you?"

"Yes sir. It's a short ride back to my place," I answer.

"No way. You are having surgery and I want you to call someone to come and pick you up."

Maybe this is more serious than I thought. More than just a biopsy. I call Janet, my voice even shakier and Janet agrees to pick me up and she'll bring Jackie who can help load my bike into the car.

In the process of the surgery, he took out a piece of my forearm about the size of a toonie and right down to the muscle. I was conscious the whole time although they wouldn't let me watch. I figured they didn't want me puking into an open wound. The whole procedure took an hour and I was 'cured.' I knew I was cured by the relieved comments the doctor made when he discovered there were no tendrils (his word) going into the muscle.

I called Janet and waited for her outside. We went to the pharmacy in the same building to buy special dressings to use at home to keep the wound wrapped. The nurses had given me a demonstration on how to wrap the surgical site.

My loving wife and daughter got me home and installed in my Lazy Boy and I rested the better part of that day, with my bike stowed in the garage. I was in shock since it all had happened so suddenly. One day I'm a healthy man and the next I am a cancer victim.

The next day I felt a little better and decided to join Janet and Jackie on a garage sale expedition. Big mistake. My emotions were so fragile that after two stops, I insisted they take me home. I could not handle the sensory input of something as simple as going to garage sales.

At the second garage sale, I scored a stereo system for twenty bucks. Now I could connect our turntable to the amplifier and speakers I had just bought. It was a simple matter to hook it all up and I could listen to my favourite vinyl, in my Lazy Boy, which comforted me.

My buddy Roy was understanding when I told him that we would have to postpone our bikepacking adventure until I healed. So much of my arm had been removed that there was still an open wound that would not close up. Having been bikepacking in the wilds before, I knew that it usually is a less than hygienic environment and I didn't want to have to deal with an infection on top of everything else.

Roy and I did make the trip after the wound had closed enough to be covered simply with a bandage. When I look at photos of that trip, I can see visible changes in myself over the course of the week we spent in the woods. A photo taken at the beginning of the trip shows me looking diminished. My helmet is askew and I am hunched over the handlebars of my bike. Yet in a photo Roy took of me five and a half days later in the Myra Canyon, I look engaged. My camping gear is stacked neatly on my bike and my helmet is fitting properly. My legs are firm. I look as I always look on these trips I make with Roy. Healthy. Strong.

It never surprises me how quickly the body will adapt to physical exertion. The very bikepacking trip that I was nervous about taking is one of the very things that helped to heal me. My recovery was shortened by the love and support of my family. Just like when we went through hard times and had lost everything, we discovered we had all we needed: Love.

15 Finding Peace

It took seventeen years after his interment for me to visit my father's grave in the historic Sutherland Cemetery outside of our hometown of Mooretown. I had been back to Ontario many times in between, most notably the one hundredth anniversary of the Donnelly massacre but I never seemed to make it to his resting spot. Going there would unleash too many sad memories.

Yet on this particular trip, my twin, my wife Janet and our infant son Christopher were visiting Mooretown, with the express goal of visiting his grave. This would have been around 1985. Driving through town, Chris and I were engaged animatedly pointing out the houses where we had delivered newspapers, and those of our friends and the more colourful characters that were our neighbours. We had stopped by our family house on Emily Street, regaling Janet with pranks from our childhood. Our two-room school house had been converted into a museum; we visited all that it had to offer in half an hour, enjoying the coolness of its interior. We had gone down to the St. Clair River and the municipal dock where we climbed to the top of the gravel pile that was always to be found there. For my brother and I, it had been a real "best of" visit.

Janet and I had planned this trip to Ontario the past winter. And I had thought, what better time to visit my father, now that I was a married man and a father myself.

The real reason I had never been back to the site was that always, in the back of my mind, there was a feeling of guilt that I have carried since the night of his death. Admittedly, my twin and I hadn't been getting along with our father. But most of that could be chalked up to our unhappiness with the move to Toronto and the fact we were teenagers during the sixties when rebellion was all around us.

At this time of my life, back in Mooretown, I felt secure enough with my wife, twin and son present to make the visit. Finding the grave was harder than I thought. The memory of his funeral was burned into my consciousness and I felt sure that it was not far from the gate, from where his casket had been carried to the site.

It was also hard to find due to the pitifully small and unprepossessing granite marker that had only his name and his year of birth and his year of death engraved on it. Long grass obscured the stone. My anxiety was somewhat alleviated by the familiar names of the families we knew from growing up in the region, Cathcart, Dennis, Lewis, Reed that we spied on our walk.

Soon after finding his marker we stood staring at the grave and I handed my son Christopher to my twin Chris. Janet wandered away to view taller and more substantial monuments nearby. Having my 35mm camera with me, I wanted to photograph the historical plaque that I knew was up the hill from Dad.

I turned to face west so I could frame up the shot to include the St. Clair River in the background. This was easy to do since the cemetery is on a hill overlooking the blue green waters of this part of the St. Lawrence Seaway.

Walking back to the grave, I could see my brother staring down at the stone with Dad's name on it. The sight of him holding my son made me stop in my tracks. Suddenly, it all became clear. All those years of guilt washed away, melted from my existence. I realized that our father still lived. Not physically. But his spirit lived on through me, that man over there who looked like me, and the toddler in his arms. We hadn't killed him after all.

They say a moment's inspiration is worth a lifetime of experience. I am a very lucky man to have experienced it. My twin didn't share that same enlightenment and it took years for my brother and my mother to patch up their relationship. Eventually they were very close and more like very good friends than just a son and mother.

This past summer, my brother and I revisited both our mother and our father's graves with our wives. A cemetery appears to be a static place yet things had changed. One can barely see the river for all the growth lower down the hill from the cemetery. And in fact, I was surprised at the meagre height of the spot. In my imagination, the hill where the cemetery rests, is a lot higher. Over to the right, Leach's Hill where we tobogganed in the winter as children is now a deep green field of soybeans. The grand tombstone of the Leach family is missing a piece of its granite cross which has fallen to the ground. It looks much like a forgotten sled at the bottom of their hill. Somehow it looks appropriate lying there, in this desolate, poorly-kept country graveyard.

A loud speed boat passes up the river going north. Its sound disturbs the whistling of the cicadas in what is usually a silent space. We wait for the boat to appear from behind the barn that hides our view of the St. Clair River. We catch a quick glimpse of the boat before it is once again hidden by the lush Ontario foliage. Then we turn our attention back to Mom and Dad's graves.

We have brought flowers to place between their stones and my idea was to have a conversation with them while we sipped from the whiskey I brought for the occasion. But I find I'm too choked up to say much. I wanted to tell them that we have turned out okay. That the two of us are married to the fine women standing beside us and we are family men now.

In the field to the south, four horses graze on its thin patchy cover. As we approach the fence, they draw nearer, wanting to be fed the grasses growing on our side. Their vitality is in sharp contrast to the stillness behind us. Bare patches under our feet speak of others standing here, perhaps looking for comfort while visiting loved ones at this cemetery.

Walking away from the horses we notice a grey granite cube, deeply engraved on its surface is the letter K. I explain that this is the method the cemetery uses to find plots, wanting to be sure to dig in the correct spot. I joke that we should put it on Mom's grave since her name was Kaye. My brother poopoos the idea thinking it would be disrespectful.

Seeing the cube reminds me of visiting the cemetery when we were boys. A group of men from the church were there to do some maintenance, paint fences, cut the grass and do general cleanup. At the same time, two gravediggers were working away at a plot when suddenly there was a lot of commotion. The men jumped out of the grave and refused to continue. In digging, they had cut too close to the next grave and had broken open an old casket. Curious, my brother and I ran over to see what all the fuss was about but our father intercepted us and held us back.

In an era that didn't have cellphones, someone had to walk down to the farm at the end of the road and call the minister, to see if he could come out and reassure these two men that they weren't going to be confined to the fires of hell for their mishap.

While waiting for the minister to arrive, the church men went back to their work. This allowed my brother and I to peek into the grave. The broken coffin was weathered and looked like it might have been a simple wooden box. Something white poked out of a corner. In our young imaginations, it was a skeleton. We got a disapproving look from our father, who had been distracted from painting the fence, due to our hooting and hollering that we had seen a real skeleton!

My wife, sister-in-law and brother have gathered near the cars and were soon going to become impatient with me. I gave up my search for the disturbed grave and concentrated on moving the granite cube with the "K" to Mom's grave without the others seeing me. Taking out my cellphone, I frame a shot of the letter on Mom's grave with Dad's grave beside her. I was unsure if I was going to show the photo to them later.

Driving down the narrow country lane, we rejoined the light traffic on the road, leaving Mom and Dad in peace while we admired the elaborate docks on the river each with their powerboats waiting for their owners to take them out on the water. Last night we had stayed with my sister Jay and her husband Paul in London, Ontario. Now we were on our way to visit my sister Hilary, in Chatham, Ontario. I felt secure in their matriarchal circles, surrounded by their children, their spouses and their grandchildren. Life was unfolding as it should.

16 When the Gift Hit the Fan

Every Christmas, as a family, we play what we call "The Gift-Grab Game" which involves all of us bringing wrapped gifts to the table. Using dice to determine who goes first, we start rolling our dice and when someone rolls a 7 or 11, they get to pick a gift and open it. Usually, the more extravagantly wrapped a gift is, the faster it gets chosen. My gifts are easily identified by their lame wrapping and are usually chosen last. That's not to say the gifts inside aren't desirable. My idea is to fool everyone into thinking that my poorly wrapped gifts will have crap inside too, and be happily surprised to find something nice instead.

It was while wrapping presents for this year's gift grab game that I thought to pull out the old gift. The blueish-purple wrapping was just as wrinkled and faded as when I pulled it out of my desk drawer last year. The clear tape had become that much more unstuck from the paper, threatening to cause the wrapper to spring open, revealing the gift inside.

I thought it would be a lark to take some pictures of it and post them on Facebook. Maybe I could convince my FB friends to share the post and we could all find the woman. I'd had an experience last year trying to find someone and I enjoyed 'the thrill of the hunt.'

Years ago, when Janet was pregnant with Chris, her brother Fred and his girlfriend Suzette came to live with us until they got settled in Alberta. Suzette had a cute young daughter named Michelle whose portrait I was keen to take. She proved to be a willing subject and I managed to create a beautiful set of black and white photos of her posing on our kitchen counter and outdoors in our woods.

Last year, on a trip to Vancouver with our son Chris, I brought the set of photos with me hoping I could find Suzette or Michelle and make a gift of the portraits. When Fred died of tragic circumstances, Suzette had moved to Vancouver and for about two years, we had contact with her. Then she faded away from our lives.

While in Vancouver, I thumbed through the Vancouver and area phone books and copied down all the same last names as hers and began to contact them. After a dozen calls, I was certain that I had found Michelle and left a message on her answering service. It might have sounded odd: "Hi. My name is Adrian Pearce and I'm looking for the daughter of Suzette _____. Suzette and her boyfriend Fred lived with my wife Janet and I near Edmonton in the early 1980's and I have portraits I took of Suzette's daughter, Michelle, that I would like to give away. Michelle was four at the time. Is this you? I'm in Vancouver for several days and would love to give them to you. You can reach me at the Hotel Vancouver." The oddness of a message like this is probably why I never heard back. Maybe it was her after all and there were other reasons she didn't want contact. Still I enjoyed trying to find her.

My thinking was that Vicki could be found in eastern Canada since that is where I lost touch with her forty years ago. So maybe a FB friend would share it and one of their FB friends who would share it... I had contact with my old high school chum Don Dagenais about ten years previously but we had lost touch. Other than Don, I'd had no contact with anyone from high school. Less so with anyone from cooking school. But I was still in contact with my Humber College roommate Bill Purchase and his wife Susan.

This was my post: Monday, December 18, 2017

47 years ago, I was given this Christmas gift by my girlfriend as she dumped me. I vowed never to open it.

The yellowed Cellotape (that's what it was called back then) will loosen a bit more, the corners will fray yet again and I will drag it out next season to enjoy the mystery of what lies inside.

(Photo of present on white and blue wrapping paper)

And my post was commented on Tuesday, December 19, 2017

6:43 am by message from Shannon Tyler, a radio jock from 99.3FM

Adrian! What a mystery... and story. Do you have time for a quick call from me this morning? I'd love to talk to you about your story on my show today. Is there a number I can reach u at after 10?

Before her noon show, Shannon interviewed me. It's all a blur now, I don't even remember what I said.

I hadn't had much contact with Shannon recently. The last time I saw her was when I was shooting a B-roll for a hot tub place on 99th Street. She was there with her husband. She said they were looking at buying a hot tub and this company was one of her clients.

The interview with Shannon was fun and I had forgotten how bubbly she could be. You have to be animated on radio since there are no visuals.

The interview made me feel important and fed my large ego. By not usually listening to radio at home, I missed her interview, while busily digging around for a radio I could quickly tune to her station.

Shannon and I had worked together at A-Channel when she was the host of "Wired," an excellent local entertainment show that I used to watch even before I started back in television. She worked on the main floor of the station while I worked upstairs in the Creative Department shooting commercials and promos, we had only worked on a few stories together but ran into each other all the time.

Tamara McLean, who I worked with at CITY TV, was now working at the CBC as a chase producer (chasing radio guests down.) She must have heard the interview and sent the following text to me.

Dec.19, 1:17 pm

Adrian I'm super intrigued by your mystery present! It may make a fun holiday interview on our show this week. Can we talk later about it?

Tamara knew I was a volunteer bike mechanic and when her station wanted a story to coincide with the opening of the new downtown bike lanes, she came to BikeWorks North and interviewed me there. The piece was not only fun to do, but fun to hear. When she proposed that I appear on Edmonton AM to talk about the present, with Mark Connolly (who I had worked with when I freelanced) I was amenable.

The story of the 47-Year-Old-Present takes a very different turn a few days later.

There's a small group that volunteer on Tuesday evenings at BikeWorks North, Nancy, Robert, Eduardo and myself. With the Christmas season soon approaching, we decide to get together and have a few drinks to celebrate. Janet joins us and meets the group she has heard so much about.

It is while we are sipping our drinks that Eduardo mentions that he heard me on 99.3 being interviewed by Shannon and wants to know all about the gift. I give him the Reader's Digest version of the story and it piques everyone's interest.

The next day, Janet and I are about to leave for a Christmas party at her cousin's place when Robert, who works for Canadian Press calls me and wants to write a story for the wire services. The assignment desk has given him some less than thrilling stories ideas to write but he feels my story is more compelling and I give him more detail than what he heard the previous night.

His story needs a photograph, so while Janet is putting on her coat to leave, I rush outside to take a selfie with me holding the present. I'm wearing what for me is a festive-looking sweater and I position myself on the driveway with one of our evergreen trees in the background. The wind is strong and I have to take several pics just to get one I like that includes not only the present and the evergreen but my hair in a reasonable facsimile of its usual style.

On Christmas Eve morning while getting ready to leave for Saskatoon to spend Christmas with our son, Chris, and his girlfriend, Joelle, I get a message from my Facebook friend, Linda Vich in Winnipeg:

"Merry Christmas Mike! The Winnipeg Free Press linked you up!"

This is my first indication that the story is spreading and I am pleased. I want it to continue travelling east to reach Ontario where I believe there is a good chance that someone back east might know of Vicki's whereabouts.

Two hours later, we are in Lloydminster, stopping at a restaurant to have lunch when I see a message from Roberta Bell of the CBC saying they are about to post an on-line version of the story and can they have permission to use some of my FB pictures?

If I had known what was going to happen, I would have been fussier about which pictures would be used in all the world-wide stories that were yet to follow given that the CBC web story would send the "47-Year-Old-Present" around the world.

Since the publication of the CBC web-story, I have seen pictures of me working at the Alberta Legislature (where I operate robotic cameras,) another of me looking skinny at the Gainer's strike of 1986, an amusing one of me with my friend Keith Halgren's parrot on my head and two from a photography class I attended a few years ago.

I like to poke fun at myself so I wasn't upset with the choice of photographs except some of them seemed to be out of context. Like displaying a picture of me in the control room at the Legislature while talking about my teenage years. Admittedly, the picture of the parrot on my head would have worked well with the New York Times headline: "WIFE STAYS WITH MORON WHO PUT UNOPENED GIFT FROM EX UNDER THE TREE FOR 47 YEARS."

Under the U.K. headline "HEART BROKE BLOKE KEEPS UNOPENED GIFT," a Facebook picture of me from the late seventies might have been more appropriate: Janet and I had been visiting a Humber College friend named Laurel Ridley who lived in Calgary and she took a photo of me laying on my back, resting on a log, right arm behind my head, looking wistfully off to my right. Long reddish-brown hair drapes onto the log. My beard is thick and my glasses give me a studious look. I also look sad.

The radio interviews took the story local. The newspaper story made it national and the CBC web story, (I found out later it was the most read CBC story at the time,) took it international. I spent most of Christmas doing radio, tv and print interviews, interrupting our holiday celebrations with Chris and Joelle which annoyed Chris to no end. That is why he always refers to the gift as "that stupid present," with an exaggerated eye roll.

I did chuckle after having Christmas dinner with Chris' girlfriend's family on Christmas Day, meeting them for the first time and instantly liking them. The next day, Joelle mentioned that her father did not realize I was the guy he had read about in the paper, sitting next to him at the feast her family put on that day. I at last had had my reprieve, a breath of anonymity in the swirl of media attention.

I was inundated, flattered by the attention, annoyed at my family for not wanting to drop everything so that I could bask in my fifteen minutes of fame. I felt an affinity with the news gatherers of the day. I wanted to help those that were searching for that elusive Christmas story that didn't involve lost kittens, Christmas lights or screeching children opening gifts. I also wanted to treat everyone equally so I stuck to the same story, over and over again.

My FB page received hundreds of friend requests, a small minority came from women claiming to be

Vicki. One of these stood out. My old high school chum Don (Douchebag,) had been in contact with Vicki for years. He contacted her about the story, "hey V: did you see this story about Snake?" And included a link to the National Post's website. Then she contacted me through Facebook. She mentioned that she had contacted me on messenger a year and a half earlier and I had ignored her. At the time I did not recognize her name as she had changed it when she married.

We messaged back and forth and I was pretty certain this woman was the girl who had given me the present. However, until we established a rapport, we decided to keep it secret for now. At the time, I was hoping to auction off the gift for someone else to open, with the proceeds to go to a local charity, the Christmas Bureau of Edmonton.

Ten days after New Year's, I was still receiving daily calls for interviews. But it was when a huge American Podcast wanted to do an episode on Janet, I put a stop to the carnival. I was concerned about where they would go with this story. At Christmas we had experienced a Boston TV station asking me to leave the room so they could ask her questions; questions like, "now Janet, be honest with us. With your husband out of the room, tell us and be honest, in all the years you have been together, haven't you opened the present?"

Janet's answer was an honest one, "I've never opened it. I don't snoop in his stuff and he doesn't snoop in mine. Besides, he keeps it in the basement and if you saw our basement, you'd know that you could never find where he hides anything!"

I didn't want to expose Janet to questions that she might be uncomfortable with or could be taken out of context and make her feel bad. I wanted to protect

her. And it was only then that I told her I had found
Vicki.

17 Erasing the Years, Part 1, by Vicki Allen

---- Original Message ----
From: Don
To: Vicki
Cc: Adrian (Mike) Pearce
Sent: Sun, Dec 24, 2017 8:34 am
Subject: Vicki... ARE YOU STILL AT THIS ADDI?
Vicki… If you are still at this email, check out this story about SNAKE:
http://nationalpost.com/news/canada/man-keeps-unopened-christmas-gift-from-girl-who-dumped-him-almost-50-years-ago
Cheers
Don

24 Dec 2017, at 12:19 PM, Vicki replied all:
OH.MI.GAWD.
Um, yes; yes, I am.
And I'm a little behind in answering emails — I adore you, Don, for not giving up on me.

You have totally made my year; possibly even the last decade just immensely improved.

Oh, wait... did I miss the point?

Hey there, Mike! I'm in B.C. now. I'm delighted — no, I'm awestruck. And thank you for what is a most wonderful gift, not being forgotten, especially at this time of year.

Shit. No clue where to start to catch up... or even if that's appropriate.

Nearly 50 years? Just... wow. Maybe two brownie points off for that reminder, but ALL the brownie points for perseverance, self-control, determination and an awesome wife (I might have tossed it that first year, yanno'?).

V.

---- Original Message ----
From: Don
To: Vicki
Sent: Sun, Dec 24, 2017 9:24 am
Subject: Re: Vicki... ARE YOU STILL AT THIS ADDI?

I received a bounce back on his email address.

Not sure how to reach him. Perhaps through the journalist who wrote the story?

Don

24 Dec 2017, at 12:42 PM, Vicki wrote:

He has a FB page, but I cannot comment on it. I did like the post about the article and the photographs.

Oh, Don; this old woman thanks you for reminding me we were all young (and some of us more foolish than others) once!

Yes, my reply bounced back for me, too.

How much nerve do I have as far as contacting the journalist? Let's see if he checks the "like" statuses and figures it out; give him a day (week?) or two.

And in the meantime, I am very glad that you are both the men that you promised to be even way back then... steadfast and dear, even now.

I may not stop grinning for quite some time!

Wish I could remember what's in that wrapping paper.

Now, I'm actually laughing somewhat like a lunatic... sheesh!

I turn 62 on Tuesday. But today? You made it possible for me to be, or at least remember how it felt to be 16 again. Yeah. You rock.

Love and hugs,
V.

---- Original Message ----
From: Don
To: Vicki
Sent: Tue, Dec 26, 2017 7:57 am
Subject: Re: Vicki... ARE YOU STILL AT THIS ADDI?

Another friend sent me the same story, but in The Star; more current picture of Snake though.

https://www.thestar.com/news/world/2017/12/25/man-keeps-unopened-christmas-gift-from-girl-who-dumped-him-almost-50-years-ago.html

Happy Birthday, kiddo. Mine is today, too — 64 — GAK!

To being mentally 16 again!
Don

[Phone ringing]
Lori: *Happy birthday, V!*
V: *Thanks! How was your Christmas?*

Wonderful; just finished packing up the leftovers for the girls to take home with them. Yours?

Lovely and quiet; got to read and chat on the phone with my family members — the ones who didn't simply text me! The last Christmas with most of them around, I had stockings filled and gifts, with dinner ready at 2 p.m. and none of them showed up until after 7 p.m., already stuffed to the gills from their friends' houses. This year? No leftovers because I didn't even cook. Yay!

No fair! You're missing the work and expense!

<laughing> Pretty much! I mailed packages; that was expensive enough! So, I was wondering... have you seen anything online about some guy not opening his ex-girlfriend's Christmas gift to him about 47 years ago?

My husband was just talking about that! He saw it on the news here. He said there are a lot of red flags raised by it. Who does that?

Um...

IF she's even still alive, what if she doesn't want her high school years thrown in her face or some guy who may still be carrying a torch for her showing up on her doorstep? Why would he save it? It seems creepy and pretty weird to hold a grudge that long. What if he's dangerous? And now people are looking for her?

Um...

Why would his wife put up with that? Is he still angry? Social media brings all the crazies out; what if somebody decides to get revenge for what she did to him?

I hadn't thought about that.

Most people don't, but you know my husband sees the other side of things like this.

I need to rethink things.

YOU? Why do you...? No.
<silence>
No, wait, that's not... omigawd, it is.
Yeah, it is. I was thinking it was showing determination and character and...
And we were thinking it suggests something more sinister. WHAT ARE YOU GOING TO DO?
I don't know. I already liked some of the photos on his FB post.
Be careful. Just... be very, very careful. And make sure you don't give out any personal information to ANY body with regards to this. Might be best to sit on it for a while.
Probably too late. But I will keep you posted if something new comes up!

Then something new did come up...
Direct Message on Messenger from Adrian (Mike) Pearce
12/26/2017 9:32pm
Tell me something from high school that only you and I would know.
To which I obliquely replied:
12/26/2017 9:56pm
Dear Karma Facilitator: I've got some deadlines to meet before potentially unleashing the hounds of media hell... hoping late tomorrow provides a decent window. Signed, with laughter, Canada's most notorious bitch.

18 The Big Lie

The story of the 47-Year-Old-Gift involved a lot of lying. Fibbing. Not telling the truth. Stretching it as though it was a piece of chewing gum.

This past Easter, Janet and I flew to Vancouver Island to visit Janet's sister (another) Vicki and her husband Glenn. Our secret agenda was to meet up with Victoria, (the person I think is the one who gave me the present.) Upon arriving, the first question Vicki (the sister) asks me is, "have you found the girl yet?" I tell her the same story I have told anyone asking that question, "there are three women claiming to be her and I'm still checking them out."

I've heard that if you are going to lie, then the lie should contain a kernel of truth. We were on Vancouver Island to visit with Vicki and Glenn and also to visit Victoria (Vicki Allen) to confirm that she was the "real" Vicki from my past. We were pretty certain she was and we spent a lot of time and effort to arrange the meeting.

My sister and brother-in-law knew that during our visit, one of our plans was to meet up with an old friend. We have made up a story that our friend lives in Duncan, a city north of Victoria, where they live. We chose Duncan since we do have two friends who live there. Again, you have to have the element of truth in your BS.

Glenn, being his usual friendly self begins to fire questions at us, "where in Duncan are you meeting your friend? Do you need directions? What time are you meeting? Glen knows Vancouver Island well from working there so long. I know the island from living on it in the nineties (another story,) and I gave him credible answers. It is my own guilt about lying that makes me suspicious of his questions. Does he know something? Can he tell we are fibbing?

Surprise, surprise, the day after meeting Victoria, my in-laws want to take us for a drive. Surprising because they want to go exactly where we had been the day before on our clandestine rendezvous; to a small place outside of Victoria. We had to pretend that we had never seen the sights before. We oooed and awed at various things they pointed out (that we had seen just yesterday!) my anxiety rose when we approached the very same pub where we had met Victoria. What if they wanted to take us there for lunch? What if we got the same server and she said something like, "back so soon?" How would we cover that?

As far as my own family, I did not tell my children the secret until this fall. With his Ragnar the Trader business, our son is a frequent visitor to Edmonton, either with shows in town or passing through for shows elsewhere. We often have dinner and a games night together, me sipping wine while he prefers Scotch and Janet, enjoying a martini.

The conversation inevitably turns to the 47-Year-Old-Present and his patience on hearing about it again and again was wearing thin. I finally let him know that we had found Vicki and of our plans to auction off the gift, to be opened by someone else.

After he left, my wife pointed out that if I was comfortable telling Chris about it then surely, I should share the same information with our daughter, Jackie who lives with us. So, I told her. We still hadn't told any other family members, Janet's twin, her large family, my sisters, or any of our close friends.

On a recent phone call with my twin, he once again launched into a paranoid fantasy. A fantasy that I was responsible for planting into his mind years ago after getting dumped and then throwing the present under the Christmas tree. He bought into my story about Wolfie being in a motorcycle gang.

"Mike, Mike, you've got to be careful," Chris pleaded with me. "You could be opening up something that doesn't want to be opened!"

I try to interrupt "What if I..."

"You haven't found her because she is dead. Or locked away somewhere. You remember those calls you made looking for her and you got a message that said, "this number does not receive incoming calls?"

He sounded desperate. I already knew there was no danger since I had found her and was trying to establish a relationship with her after forty years. We were spending some time together through messaging and phone calls, finding out about each other's lives.

Sensing his distress, I interrupt him.

"What if I told you I found her?"

Silence.

"Are you still there?" I ask tentatively.

After a long pause, he speaks. "What are you talking about?"

"I'm trying to tell you that I have found her. I am pretty sure it is her."

Soon after being ditched, to make myself feel better, I made this Wolfie person out to be an Alpha male. An older, sexier, streetwise, motorcycle-riding macho man. With his character being so large in my mind, I could keep my pride. How could a short, skinny nerd like me compete for Vicki's affections up against this type of competition? My friends would all console me, "we understand, man. You didn't stand a chance. We wouldn't stand a chance against a guy like that either."

Over the decades, this story has grown like a disease in my brother's mind. It had grown new roots by my having posted about the gift and the story going viral. And now he also knows that I am writing a book about it, with the idea of publishing the book.

My twin is furious that I hadn't told him and I reminded him that he had given me some advice once. I had told a coworker in confidence how much money I made and she went and blabbed that to another coworker who was making less and there was hell to pay. I was living in a world of self-inflicted pain. My relationship with both coworkers was never the same again. His advice to me? "if you don't want someone to know something, don't tell anyone."

So now you, Dear Reader, you know that I lied to the whole world. Well, technically, I didn't lie, I just withheld some of the information. It was just a little, tiny, white lie. Well not a lie exactly, more like a fib, you know...to keep everyone happy.

19 The Meeting

We are staying in Victoria with Victoria to meet Victoria who lives near Victoria. That is how we find ourselves outside, at a pub on this Easter weekend. The search for the 'girl' who gave me the present is very close to being completed. We wouldn't have spent a thousand dollars and travelled eight hundred miles to meet her if we weren't sure it was the Vicki Allen I dated so long ago.

It had been agreed that we would all meet at this pub near where Victoria lives to "establish a neutral comfort zone for Janet," (using Victoria's words,) before driving to Victoria's home, some distance away and that is apparently hard to find.

We arrive even before the pub opens after a short drive from the city of Victoria where we are staying with Janet's sister, another Vicki and her husband Glenn. They have very kindly lent us their van on the pretext that we are meeting an old friend in a place up island called Duncan. My sister-in-law, like everyone else thinks that I'm still looking for the 'girl' so we had to fib as to our real destination. As an aside, my sister-in-law Vicki was contacted by a stranger asking if she was the one who gave me the gift.

The pub is a Tudor styled structure that sits very near to the road. It is so close that it is a wonder that a vehicle hasn't crashed into it. The pub was once a stagecoach stop on the long journey to the mineral deposits at this part of Vancouver Island. That might explain its proximity to the road.

Nervously standing at the front door, I scan the small group of people that are also milling around the parking lot waiting for the place to open. What about that couple over there? Did she bring someone along for security? What about that woman leaning against the handrail. Could that be her?

What I fail to realize after all the preparations and plans to meet, is that I had forgotten to actually set a specific time. In her last text, Victoria said any time after eleven. I never confirmed it. Once the doors open (at eleven,) we choose a booth in the back of the pub and wait. I text her that we are here and I get an instant response, "oh shit! I'll be there shortly!"

"You Really Got a Hold on Me" by Smokey Robinson plays softly in the background amid the clatter of plates and cutlery, as the pub readies itself for another day. I think about how this story really has a hold on me while we wait. Janet insists that I sit and the head of the table so that I can be between her and Victoria, in the 'power seat.' Knowing both these women, I don't think that will be necessary. This isn't a confrontation. Yet in spite of her calm demeanour, Janet may be just a little nervous about meeting a woman I dated in the past. Even if that past was forty-seven years ago and the two of us have had no contact in forty years.

Janet and I have talked about this at great length. I want to be sure this whole "47-Year-Old-Present" thing is not going to be a problem for my wife of thirty-eight years. Janet, who is a writer, thinks that this is a good story. She knows I have no romantic feelings for anyone else. She is confident in our relationship.

The only discord came when I locked the present into our fire safe. "So, the children's baby pictures can all go up in flames but that damn present will be spared!" she commented.

Thirty minutes later, a woman clothed head to toe in purple enters the room. I don't recognize her yet logical deduction tells me that this is Vicki. I stand up to greet her and give her a hug. "Please don't do that!" she says. I have to remember that not everyone is a hugger. Although she gives Janet a hug; two in fact. When I point this out, she responds, "eat your heart out!"

Sitting down, she tells us that she had no time to prepare since she wasn't expecting us at eleven. She admires Janet's nails which Janet playfully hand-models for her. Victoria details the comments that her local girlfriends and those in South Carolina have made about our meeting. Things like: "what are you going to wear?" Or "what about his wife?" and "are you actually going to bring them into your home?"

I find out later, when Janet has gone to the lady's room, and Victoria, (which is how she prefers to be called) says to me, "do you have an axe under the table? And you and your accomplice are going to murder me?" that she is truly paranoid of our intentions. At first, I think that she is joking. Then she explains that she makes her living transcribing parole hearings for several prisons and has heard all kinds of horrible things. "I'm still trying to get over my fear," she tells me. It occurs to me that this woman has had a difficult time of it living in South Carolina and raising a family on her own.

Janet comes back to the table and starts taking pictures. "I hate having my picture taken," says Victoria.

"You always have," I point out, getting a wry smile. I guess a comfort level has been reached and I relax.

I think back to all the times I have photographed this woman. I was the president of our high school camera club when we dated. She does look different after all these years. Gone is the Roman nose that I always liked. Gone as well is the cute gap between her front teeth. Almost as if reading my thoughts, she asks me if I remember taking photos of her face before she had rhinoplasty. I do remember that.

When the server approaches, Victoria asks her if she knows what the story we are meeting over is about. When she says she has no idea, we shut down that line of discussion and order our meals. Victoria tells us not to order the "Maple Leaf" poutine as it is an in-house joke. Janet gets a wrap and I order a chicken salad. "Healthy choices," she notes as she orders a regular poutine.

We explain to Victoria that we are keeping it secret that we have found her. Our children don't know. Even Janet's sister and her husband that we are staying with don't know. We tell her that we have fabricated a story about our whereabouts this day.

We leave the parking lot of the pub and Victoria drives at a much faster speed than I do. I am in my brother-in-law's van and want to be extra careful. I have trouble keeping her in sight. And it is just as well I do keep an eye on her car. The road twists and turns sharply. Suddenly she makes a right into a hidden driveway. I brake quickly and find that she wasn't kidding. I never would have found this place. Has she chosen a hidden-away place for a reason?

It looks exactly like a photo on her Facebook page but because the house is hidden from the road, I doubt I could have found it on my own. It is a well maintained two-storey and her apartment is on the ground floor. When she opens her door, two dogs emerge. The black and white one must be Hoochie Mama and the darker dog Emmylou, her long-time boyfriend's dog from South Carolina. She calls her ex "The Warden" for complicated reasons. He has since passed and now she is alone.

After a short tour, I go to put the six pack of beer I brought along in the fridge. It turns out that Victoria is not a drinker. And when I think about it, I cannot recall ever drinking with her. Smoking, yes. Drinking, no.

Victoria chooses to sit on a chair facing us as we both are sitting side by side on her couch. Janet asks about the quilt on the back of the couch and is told that it is made from "The Warden's" t-shirts. The quilt smells vaguely of aftershave and immediately I inch my back away so I am not touching it. The thing creeps me out a little.

Victoria gets up to rummage through a pile of Rubbermaid containers stacked up in a corner of her living room. I get up to help lift the bins and see that they are full of papers - not much different than the countless boxes I have in my own basement. One of them contains artwork from her four children. She tells us that she needs to downsize all this material gathered over 62 years. We understand perfectly.

From one of the tubs, Victoria pulls out a 1971 George S. Henry yearbook. I am eager to check it out-not having one of my own. Hating high school so much, I never saved many mementos from that period and I am excited thinking that the book's contents will fill in many of the gaps in my memory of that period.

Sitting beside Victoria on the couch, I look at her hands to see if I recognize them. I don't. Would she recognize my sixty-four-year-old hands? Does she recognize me at all? I'm still having difficulty recognizing her. Although I do like her hair. While it is grey now, it is still basically the same style as when we were dating. As evidenced from a photo of the camera club of that year, my hair is quite a lot shorter now than back then. While alive, our father never let us grow our hair over our ears. After his death, both my twin and I let our hair grow long.

Hoisting the yearbook off the coffee table, old report cards flutter onto our laps. This should be good, I think to myself. Yet I am shocked by her teacher's comments: "Vicki is a bright student and if she showed up to more classes, she would do well. Or this one: "If she applied herself in English class, I would give her top marks."

"What did your parents think of these?" I ask.

"I could forge my father's signature perfectly!" She brags.

"What are all these comments about attendance? I ask.

She sticks her tongue out at me.

Janet is amused and tells Victoria about the many times she skipped school and spent her time at the National Museum in Ottawa. I can see that these two are getting along just fine. Getting along so well that when Victoria needs to go outside for a smoke, Janet, a non-smoker, joins her.

As I thumb through the year book, I can see the two of them chatting comfortably through the large living room window. While I wasn't a hundred percent sure of what to expect when these two met, they sure seem to be hitting it off. I am pleased. In the autographs section of the yearbook, I come across a long scrawl written by hand that fills one page and extends to another:

I find it interesting to note that as I write this, that I have written over two dozen love letters this morning to two dozen girls I don't even know: could it be that I am popular or that I am paranoid. Probably paranoid since I just had a look at myself in the mirror...But remember me not as the paranoid freak that I am but rather as the all-American boy who is so mixed up that he is turned into a homicidal killer of young dreams. Henceforth unto this point I shall refer to you as Vicki rather than the alias of Ricky, Randy etc. Please let me apologize for any problems or past worries I may have caused in the past and I have turned over a new leaf in my life and shall discontinue all unsolicited insults on the fairer sex. Let this also be my letter of resignation from the position of president of midnight industries, also I wish to be known by the name Don rather than "Vince" or any other phony name I may have used in the past. With this I shall join a monastery and become a monk for the rest of my days. (I heard these monks have a whale of a time with the nuns.)

May your relationship with Mike last forever and be a deep one.

Best wishes for now and always

Donnie

Maybe this explains how they have managed to stay in touch over the decades.

Hoochie Mama sits quietly on an ottoman by the window and I appreciate her manner. I was concerned that Victoria's dogs would be those yappy, in-your-face types that would constantly interrupt our meeting. The fact that the two dogs are complacent tells me something about their owner. What it tells me I'm still not sure.

When the two of them come back in, Victoria sits next to me again and asks, "Do you remember the breakup?"

"I remember you coming up to me while I was having a smoke across from the school and handing me the present then telling me that you couldn't go out with me anymore."

"I know I told you about my interest in another boy. But I never told you the real reason."

I brace myself. There is more? Another reason she left me?

"I was shopping with Christine at Yorkdale Mall for your Christmas present when we could see a guy approaching us. He was holding mistletoe over his head and when he got close enough, he put his arms around me, bent me backwards and gave me a huge kiss."

I interrupt, "that's not so bad!" Then she comes to the real reason she dumped me. "Yes, it was because I kissed him back so passionately that I knew I couldn't continue on with you. I had to break up. I couldn't see two guys at the same time and I also knew that Christine would tell you and that would break us up anyway."

"Holy shit! Did I know this and have forgotten it!?

"No. I never told you the whole story. I knew you would be hurt more if I had told you."

"Wow! This changes everything. All those people who left nasty, judgmental comments about you on social media, if they only knew the whole story, they'd look at you differently."

"Well, it's a little late for that. They think I am Canada's worst bitch!"

My mind boggles at this information. Not only does she have integrity, also she was caring enough to not hurt my already trampled feelings any more than necessary.

"Had you already bought the gift?" I ask, still thinking about this new information.

"Yes. And I took it home and wrapped it and gave it to you the next day."

"Do you remember what's inside of it?" I'm hoping she doesn't remember as I'm not sure I want to know.

"I have no idea. Remember, I was working as a cashier at Canadian Tire and making a dollar twenty-five an hour. Like one of the comments in the Globe and Mail: "It (the gift) probably still has the $2.99 sticker on it!"

Vicki dumping me must have had a greater effect on me than I have ever acknowledged. According to Victoria, after the breakup, Don Dagenais and I followed her to the Royal Ontario Museum, she had just happened to meet a fellow there and they walked out together. And that is when I completely lost my shit, thinking this guy was Wolfie.

I don't remember this but I don't doubt it happened. There was one time I do remember, running around the neighbourhood near Christine's house. The three of us, Douchebag, Toolbag and myself armed ourselves with rolls of pennies in our fists. Christine had mentioned that Wolfie was coming over to her place to meet Vicki.

We ran outside and made a big production of pretending to be chasing the guy and beating him up. It was rather ridiculous. Yet it must have been due to my jealousy of being dumped, my male pride. Don and Steve must have still been dating Christine and Terri so here I was the only one of the trio having been dumped. I was hurting.

Looking through her picture window, we can see the early spring sun falling behind the island's mountains to the west. It is getting late in the day.

"Let's go outside. I want to show you something," Victoria says, standing up. I can only imagine what new surprise awaits me outside.

We only step a few yards away, not even far enough for her to have let the dogs out of the apartment, before she is pulling open a garage door. Inside sits a sports car. An MG. Is this the same MG that she owned when I saw her forty years ago? The one that was in storage when I met her seven years after the breakup and we had to take a station wagon to get back to my apartment, 'The Dive at 265?'

The MG belonged to 'The Warden.' Dust covers its contours like a blanket. The interior is a mess; strands of wire poke out of the dashboard. Just like the present I think. She's holding onto her past and the item she is holding is tattered, falling apart. Who am I to judge? The present I have been dragging around for decades is tattered and falling apart. What does all this mean?

We soon have to drive back to Victoria (the city) and see Vicki and Glenn. They might begin to worry about us and God knows we have bull-shitted them enough already. We do stop for dinner in Victoria and plot out our story, just to make sure we both have the story straight. I'm a little in shock, still thinking about meeting Victoria (the gift-giver) and all that I have learned while seeing her. It is a little overwhelming.

To think that after forty-seven years, I finally know why she dumped me back in high school.

20 Erasing the Years, Part 2, By Vicki Allen

Even 30 years ago, Mike would've been unlikely to find me.

That he did is a frightening demonstration of the power and scope of social media.

Despite carefully crafting a recitation of specific and, to me, noteworthy occurrences between the two of us, Mike maintained his skepticism about my claim to be the gift-giver until I forwarded to him the email from Don that first brought it to my attention. It took only a couple of days for the internet to do what it does best: turn over rocks, expose people to the light, and possibly even inform or entertain those who seek knowledge or connections.

In my defense, I rarely watch television or listen to the radio; I spend a lot of time at my computer engaged in work and happily stay away from monitors and audio when not editing or transcribing. "Quiet" is my happy place after raising four children over 36 years. I removed myself from the bosom of my family because I had not lived as much else other than an indentured servant and general dogsbody since I was twenty-four. Distance was the only way to stop being fully engaged in trying to run my children's lives. Not that I've given that up over such a minor inconvenience, but the intent was there.

I refer to it as "emanciparenting." I suspect the children refer to it as "Mom's lost her mind." But it was time; time to spend perhaps my last ten years doing what I want, where I want, and making my own rules and paradigms to suit myself, not the ravening hordes.

And now... suddenly I'm drowning in my own high school drama. Forty-seven years after the fact.

They wanted to meet up with me.

That phone conversation with my girlfriend had me on edge. Those were all valid points she brought up; my vanity had eclipsed my common sense in my initial reaction. What if there was rage or, at the very least, anger still in the mix? What if Mike's wife decided I was a problem that needed to be solved, much as that gift should have been tossed into the fireplace? And on a whole different level, what if meeting Mike again after all these years simply made me unsatisfied with the choices I made and the decisions that have created my reality? The upside to opening the door to nostalgia wasn't exactly overwhelming me with good juju.

He called. More than once. His voice sounded the same; familiar, unthreatening; his words reasonable and possibly measured, much as I suspect he carefully placed a timer for an hour when he did make contact. An old woman who lives alone with little social life tends to talk. A lot.

Mike and his wife, Janet, made plans, plans to meet with me and plans to use the unopened gift as a fundraiser for a good cause. My rigorously sought-after isolation and insulation were at risk, and, after decades of living in the United States, vulnerability seemed to be a real issue to me. I sought an ally and a safe place so that if we did meet, I would have witnesses to any outcome. Could've saved myself the effort, though.

Their visit snuck up on me.

Dilemma #1: What do you wear to meet with people who may be axe murderers?

Dilemma #2: What if Janet, Mike's wife, hates me on sight?

Dilemma #3: What exactly is a safe place and how do I insist on it when I seem to be the only person without any input on what happens next, since someone I no longer know is now determining how my life is affected going forward?

Dilemma #4: I don't suffer from anxiety. I am now suffering from anxiety. Mostly because of dreading public opinion, especially through social media, on a mass scale, knowing how easily it gets ugly. How do I stay reclusive and... safe?

There's a local establishment where I will watch an occasional hockey game on a Saturday night, since I do not have cable TV. Most of the staff know me, but the day we arranged to meet there, Marina, our waitperson, had no reason to remember me from any of the hundreds of people she's served in the past couple of years. So much for an ally.

I was late, happily waiting to have an exact time confirmed when it was assumed the only time mentioned was sufficient. Already awkward and proving myself inconsiderate, I rushed into the building, then reminded myself that my dignity was definitely in question so it could use a little bolstering at this point. Ohm. Breathe. Walk with decorum.

And there they both were; two at a table for six, Mike easily recognizable despite all the years since I last saw him. I looked around in case there was a chance that others had come with them (to record the event? to turn into an angry mob seeking vengeance? to pull me up short if my body language suggested I was prevaricating or outright lying?). Nope. Just us, a table for six, and two or three other empty tables in a fairly secluded room. Suddenly I could exhale and simply take this most unusual re-introduction for what it was... a chance to re-align some stars while creating a silver lining to what may have been nighttime clouds in Mike's high school years.

There were early moments of trifling small talk, as we sorted out who we were versus who we are. Janet, whose background was entirely unknown to me, was kind and generous with information that established her very firmly as a woman quite independent of being "just" a wife and mother.

Unusually enough, there was no glossing over any of our warts or wows; none of us felt the need to brag or apologize for having experienced rich and full lives that had seen plenty of highs and the occasional low. I was charmed. And I relaxed. But I did not forget that, in light of their intentions to use the 47-Year-Old-Gift to benefit charity, Mike's expertise in scripting was fully directed toward calling the shots once he set the stage. I did agree with the need to keep things on the down-low over our meeting, not that I can easily lie when asked a direct question as I tend to stammer once I get past the deer-in-the-headlights stage. But, after all, it was in my best interests not to keep the spotlight on the headline, even if I did argue that the best time to make the biggest splash was while awareness of the topic was top of mind.

Did I miss any clichés in that last paragraph?

We clicked, Janet and I, thinking much along the same lines and having reached that welcome stage in life where being blunt is much easier than worrying about people's feelings. To reach that stage of comfortable conversation with someone you've just met is rare and always welcome.

Mike, annoyingly enough, remembered much more of our high school days than I did, as he had the advantage of having had many conversations in the previous four months to twig memories and connect random dots. I had mentally avoided dealing with much but the worry of daily watching for a CBC camera truck hauling ass up my driveway with "Eureka! We found her," being screamed from the cab.

Janet generously bought lunch. Marina was hopeful we would indulge in dessert, but after I asked if their vehicle's trunk would pass a luminol check (I was kidding; swear!), I felt confident enough in their company to invite Mike and his wife back to my apartment where I knew, with just a bit of digging, I could find the high school yearbook that featured the Camera Club president's main subject in my junior year — me, the gawky, too self-conscious teenager who hated having her photo taken but somehow managed to be on nearly every page of that damn book. Okay, maybe there were only about eighteen photos of me in it, but Mike had written on just about every page plus the inside covers... it was only during this visit that I learned most of those flattering snippets of poetry were stolen lyrics from '70's music best forgotten. Add "gullible" to my self-description, sigh.

And yet, it was lovely. We wallowed, with Janet graciously witnessing us reminiscing about innocent times that we would never know again, recalling people whose lives touched ours and whose lives, perhaps, we made more of an impression on than we gave ourselves credit over.

I admit that I did not understand the depth of Mike's feelings for me. I only knew that, while I enjoyed his company and our tentative explorations into boyfriend/girlfriend territory, I was also pretty sure that there was a world of experiences beyond high school that called to me, and thought perhaps that only I heard that voice.

On that Monday in April 2018, when Mike, Janet and I met, the six of us in the Camera Club were somehow once again fifteen and seventeen; an unexpected blessing of being immersed in memories that grew more vivid as we walked those old hallways of George S. Henry Secondary School in our minds.

May our renewed and new friendship help keep us young.

21 Six Degrees of Separation, by Jan Piers

The saying goes that with six or less steps of personal associations, all of us are connected. When I met Victoria, an immediate bond was forged. We hugged and exchanged compliments. I am sure that had I met Victoria on her own, neither of us suspecting our connection through Mike, then we would have become instant friends, as I think we did, despite our one degree of separation through him.

I thought Victoria was a brave soul, moving to British Columbia after living most of her adult life in South Carolina. Her demeanor is all Vancouver Island. She is a warm and well-spoken individual. Well read, with a quirky sense of humour, Victoria is in touch with what's hip and what's happening in the world and yet is laid back and is embracing a slower pace of life. I love that mixture of the bohemian and the cosmopolitan.

We meet at an old coach house inn, reputed to be haunted by one of its previous owners. "She plays tricks on us," reports our waitress when we ask about it. The pub sits right alongside the highway, yet once inside its ancient and dark interior, you forget about the road as we neither hear traffic nor can spot it from any of its windows.

We sit in a back room, the only occupants. Across the room from us there is a large fireplace, unlit, and beyond it, a bright, sunny view of the gardened patio. It is the first of April, very early spring. We had departed a snow-covered Edmonton to meet Victoria, and the island offers us a lovely green delight. I can only imagine its wild, overgrown and colorful gardens come summer.

Victoria and Mike chat about their teen years and small snippets of their lives since they left high school. They talk about friends they shared way back when and what they know of their lives today. It was one of these who actually linked them once the story of the 47-Year-Old-Gift went viral last Christmas. I snap a few photos of the two of them while we wait for our meals.

My own family moved a lot when I was a teenager, I think I attended three or four high schools in as many cities across Canada, and while a lot of faces flash through my memory, I don't have any names of close friends from those years. It seems really special to me that they have connected, found common ground for conversation and were amicable with so much time having passed since that fateful Christmas.

Young love is so tender and intense. We probably all bear the searing lashes on our hearts and souls from those first romantic encounters. Most of us would not be brave enough to search out that first special person in our lives and attempt to reconnect.

Our teenage years are fraught with conflicting emotions. We want to be cool, we want to be noble, but not a goodie-goodie, we want to do right and fit in, yet be unique. And this coincides in a high school atmosphere full of jealousy, judgement, naïveté and immaturity. We are finding out about ourselves, discovering things we may not like and things we aspire to be, all the while our emerging hormones rage war with our self-control. Remember also the times, the era in which we grew up. We are the baby-boomer generation, the repressed fifties babies who came to age in the swinging sixties. It's amazing that somehow, most of us turned out okay.

Was there some trepidation on Victoria's part, building up to this meeting day, that perhaps Mike has been holding a grudge these many years over their breakup? Was she worried about how I would view her? Why would anyone hold onto a 47-Year-Old-Gift anyway?

We laughed and commiserated over our lunch and Victoria invited us back to her home at its conclusion.

From the front porch, Victoria enjoys a view over treetops of a picturesque harbour. Rabbits, deer and bears are frequent visitors to her yard. The backyard is a wooded mountainside, topped in craggy rock. As we arrive, her neighbour's large dog comes barking and bounding over to us and Victoria is quietly warning us against it. Mike is in the rear and greets it as it has covered the whole front yard before we have had a chance to make it to the door.

Immediately, it turns meek, it is all bark and no bite. It turns out to be a friendly, older dog, half-blind and perhaps half-deaf. It enters the house with us and greets Victoria's two dogs, Hoochie Mama and Emmylou. All three dogs precede Victoria to the kitchen; there is a ritual here and visitors be damned, it will be adhered to. Victoria pulls out baggies of doggie treats and dispenses them evenly. I take one of the treats and use it to lure the neighbour's dog back out the front door.

Victoria's living room is eclectic and colorful. There is a raised dog bed by the front window, Hoochie Mama settles on it to my right for a nap. Mike joins me on the couch and Victoria sits across the room. She talks about her life on the island and the places she has discovered. We are sorely tempted to leave the frozen prairie and make the move. We know the island from honeymooning here.

Victoria opens a closet and pulls out large plastic bins. The first two yield her children's mementos, school projects, artwork, medical and dental receipts. In the third bin, she discovers, to Mike's delight, their high school yearbook. I snap photos of the two of them as they take yet another stroll down memory lane. Before we leave, he secures permission from her to take it home to Edmonton with him.

After we part, and drive back to Victoria, (the city), Mike thanks me for giving up my afternoon on this pursuit. He keeps asking me what I think of Victoria (the gift-giver.) I can see he is pleased with how the day has gone and I tell him that today, I have more in common with her than he does. I believe we would be close friends if we lived near each other. I found her intelligent, witty, caring, an earth mother type full of wisdom.

People want to know from me why that 47-Year-Old-Gift still exists. Surely, with all the moves we've made, it could have gotten lost, one Christmas it might have been accidentally tossed into the fireplace or one of the children could have inadvertently opened it. I smile or chuckle, as I am doing now, writing this. One can see, looking at it, that it is just a small token gift. And I know Mike. He is eccentric. I can understand his first refusal to open the gift the year it was given. Yet it was his gift. He swore he would not open it, so his mother saved it for the next year. He kept to his word, yet it was a gift and he could not bring himself to throw it out. Over the years, it just became a joke. One Christmas, our five-year-old daughter secured a promise from him that she could open it once he died.

I like the completion of the story, that it has gone full circle. Mike and Victoria have reconnected, discussed their time together and their breakup, found they don't have much connecting them except for that absurd present, of course. They were able to regale each other with their life stories, and most important to me, because of the internet sensation, that small purple parcel will be raffled off and a Christmas charity will benefit. Someone's life will hold just a glimmer more of joy in it because of that 47-Year-Old-Gift.

22 The Big Reveal

The story still has some legs, nine months after the Facebook post. A Mexican TV station recently did a five-minute story, and I am swamped with Mexican fans. A friend tells me she has seen the story in the Coffee News here in Edmonton, then I find that newspaper in southern Alberta, and one of my Facebook friends posted to tell me she read it in Wallaceburg, Ontario, near my hometown of Mooretown.

With the season changing to fall, I decide I had better contact the Christmas Bureau of Edmonton and let them know I'd like the opening of the gift to be used to raise money for their cause. We arrange a meeting and they are prepared, having researched me and the story itself. I respect their thoroughness. They have to be careful that they don't get involved in a scam.

I meet the Executive Director, Darlene and Lee, the Events and Volunteer Coordinator, at their office on the east side. Their welcoming manner tells me that I have passed their test and after thanking me for choosing them, they ask why their charity over others. It was a simple choice for me. I have experience volunteering with another Christmas charity in our city. They have lots of volunteers and sponsors. "Your charity is considered the "little sister" and I think you could use my help more than they could," I tell them.

The date for opening the present and raising funds has to be carefully chosen. The Grey Cup is being held here, so that would not be a good time. Our event would get lost in the shuffle. The Christmas Bureau is launching their Christmas campaign on November thirteenth so that wouldn't be the ideal time either.

We decide to consider two dates, November twenty-seventh, which is the National Day of Giving, or December fourth. I like the date in December since that would give me more time to plan the event and finish the book. We agree to meet again soon and, in the meantime, look for a place to hold the event and find the 'girl.'

A week later, I am contacted by Alyson Di Franco, a senior producer of the Steve Harvey Show, based out of Los Angeles. The story has been in the back of her mind since she first heard of it last Christmas. The show is planning for the month of December to showcase Christmas-themed episodes and she wants to fly us to L.A. for an episode of the show. "Have you found the girl?" she asks. I slough off her question and she comes back to it later saying they have the resources to find her. I tell Alyson I'll have to think about that. I give her my word that we will appear on the show and I want to know when this will take place. They still have not scheduled a date.

The problem is that I already have a pretty good idea of when opening the gift will work best for the

Christmas Bureau and I worry that appearing on the Steve Harvey Show will throw a wrench into the fundraising here in Edmonton. If we open the present on their show first, how are we going to raise money for a present that has already been opened? I get a headache just thinking about it.

A week passes and I haven't heard from the Steve Harvey Show as to a date for taping. But I have heard from the Christmas Bureau; they would like me to pin down the date so that they can make plans and draw up schedules for the volunteer help we are going to need. We agree to another meeting.

At the next meeting, Darlene and Lee introduce me to Raylene who is their Special Events Coordinator. She is bubbling over with excitement about a partnership between the Bureau and the opening of the present. She is full of good ideas as to how to go about the event and raise money. Then she asks me if I have found a location to hold the fundraising present opening. I have nothing to offer and I fill them in on the Steve Harvey Show element that has been thrown into the mix.

Then Raylene gets our immediate attention by telling us that she has a third party that wants to help the Christmas Bureau. This group has a huge facility that might be suitable to hold the event. The next step is for me to meet the third party and also settle on a date that works for everyone.

After meeting with the third party, I decide that the venue is just not going to work. Janet suggests I call our friend, Gracie Jane Generoux, who owns a combination art gallery and boutique bar in downtown St. Albert, a city just on the northwest border of Edmonton.

We met her through our friends, Jack and Vern (The World Famous Peckerheads, a karaoke band)

and we have visited her establishment many times and enjoyed its unique atmosphere. What makes it unique is that every surface is covered in her artwork; tables, chairs, bottles, even the ceiling.

A year ago, I made a feature story of her that I intended to have shown on TV. In meetings I had with the CBC they expressed some interest. Gracie Jane was more than willing to have me come out to her studio at her acreage west of the city. For the story I also shot several events at her bar with an excited crowd as my backdrop. Gracie Jane is an old hand at interviews and gave me choice clips to use in the story.

Janet loved one of her paintings, and knowing that if I didn't buy it soon for her, that it would be gone for good, I gave it to her as a wedding anniversary gift and it hangs now above our bed.

Why I hadn't thought to ask Gracie Jane in the first place to use her venue for our event is beyond me. With the popularity of her boutique bar I must have thought that there would be no room in the schedule for our gift opening and book launch event.

I felt very confident striding into the place that Saturday afternoon. A small crowd had already gathered and Jessie, Gracie's daughter, was busy behind the bar. Her mother hadn't shown up to work yet so I called her on her cellphone.

Gracie Jane must have my phone number programmed into her phone as she knew it was me calling right away. After catching up, I explained my predicament and she said she would be honoured to host the event. We still had to work out the details and I was relieved that she wanted to help us.

It is good to have the love and support of my old friends.

I contact Alyson at the Steve Harvey Show and let her know we have a definite date for the gift opening here in Edmonton. She is an experienced producer and can quickly see the potential of a new angle. We open the gift here in Edmonton and have the event recorded so we can show the 'reveal' on live television with Janet, Victoria and I present. She will let me know when the date of our episode will be. This is all working out.

Epilogue - My Thoughts on Writing This Book

How do you write a book? In less than a year? This thought has been occurring to me now that our weather has gotten decent and I find I am torn between writing, cycling, working, volunteering and gardening. These are all things I want to do and have meaning for me.

For the last five years, I have participated in NaNoWriMo, National Novel Writing Month, where the challenge is to write a fifty-thousand-word novel in one month. That works out to one thousand, six hundred and sixty-seven words a day, every day. And God help you if you fall behind. One year, on the last day, when I added up my words, I discovered that I had only written forty thousand. I texted my boss and asked if I could have the next day off and I stayed home and wrote ten thousand words that day. By ten o'clock that evening, I was exhausted and completely done in, sitting at my keyboard. I'm not one for sitting around very much. It was agony to have to sit in one place and pound away on the keys all day long.

Late in the evening with only two hours to go, I uploaded my Word document into NaNoWriMo's website. Their word counter spat out a total of sixty thousand words! ... I never was very good at math. I felt everything at once, happy wonderment at having written an extra ten thousand words, anger at having spent the day trapped in a chair when I could have been doing other stuff and anxiety over missing a day of work for naught. I never want a repeat of that experience again.

But the thing is with writing fifty thousand words in one month, you are just puking it out. There is no time to concern yourself with grammatical errors, punctuation, you just want to get it down on paper. I've written about my childhood, the A-Channel Strike, bikepacking the KVR, my parents and my dreams.

I often thought that when I retired, I wanted to write a book. Thing is, I'm only semi-retired, if that is an excuse. It's not. Unlike NaNoWriMo, I have a story that given the attention it received last Christmas, is a story people want to know about.

On July fourth, 2018, at seven-thirty in the morning, I read my first chapter to Janet while we were still in bed. I have my first coffee of the day beside me on the night table. She hates it! I burst out laughing as I thought it was pretty good. Oh boy! We're in for it now! Janet is sheepish and tries to apologize for her opinion. She says, "wait until my book is done and then I'll help you write your book."

She is going through a very laborious process of publishing her own novel. It seems like she has been working on it forever. I've read the final draft. I offered some grammatical changes and some changes to the guns in her book. (She had a shotgun firing bullets and didn't know that shells get ejected from the chamber.) I also drew a map for her of the area where her story takes place, which is in the general vicinity of where our acreage was.

While she writes, I do the heavy lifting of the household chores. She gets so focused on her writing that it is as though she has disappeared. She doesn't hear her name called. She doesn't hear the phone ring. She closets herself away in her office that we refer to as the 'Green Room,' because of its bright green walls.

I make all the meals and have to negotiate with her to come and have breakfast and supper. Jackie gives her massages to ease her stiff body. Many is a night I go to bed alone. Janet is a night owl and prefers being up until two and then sleeping until ten. My pattern is almost the opposite.

It worries me when I see how much time it has taken her to publish her book and I'm supposed to have mine ready for Christmas. I'm trying to focus on writing one chapter at a time and then trying to perfect it as well as I can. However, my writing has been all over the map and I'm finding that the summer weather has been quite a distraction. There's grass to cut and gardening to do. I have two part time jobs. Most of the stories I've written recently are unfinished. Seventy-two of them in fact. Seventy-two!

And Janet tells me that we can't use all of them for the "47-Year-Old Present" book.

There is a dream from my Dream Diary from around that time:

Thursday, July 5th, 2018, Time: 3 am
Dream: "He's all over the map!"

I walk into a huge tv studio. I'm wearing an apron and walking past curved walls like the ones at A-Channel. I enter a large studio that is more like a gym. The place is full of people all wearing the same coloured t-shirts.

At the front of the studio is a large screen covered in splotches, some kind of hi-tech green screen. The studio audience is practising clapping and as I walk in front of the screen a man in the crowd stands up and says, "he's all over the map!" In each hand he holds ping pong paddles.

I realize I need help and began to read a book about writing a memoir; the author describes it as a story within the story of your life. The book suggests making stories titled: "The Time I...". So, I began writing those kinds of stories. Like "The Time I nearly Died in A Helicopter" or "The Time I fell a Hundred Feet Face first" or "The Time We Made the Pope Take a Hike."

These are all good stories but the question remains; where do they fit into the narrative? Janet and I discuss what the book, the "47-Year-Old-Present" is about, who is the target audience, and I realize not all my stories can fit into it. I conclude that I should write more of a "trailer" about my life, the highlights of the last forty-seven years. Enough to whet people's appetites.

I write a long, two-thousand-word chapter about all the pranks I have pulled or that have been pulled on me, in the past. I think it is funny but Janet argues that it has nothing to do with the 47-Year-Old-Present. She wants me to write more about the girls I dated before we were married. She wants me to describe my feelings. Can you believe it? My wife wants more details about my exes!

The feeling of being overwhelmed is strong. I'm working two part time jobs, freelancing as a cameraman, organizing a bikepacking trip, involved in a garage sale and emptying our crammed basement to renovate it. A bit much methinks. Luckily, this is about the time Janet starts picking up the slack for me.

With all the things going on at the same time, I sometimes think I am going to lose my mind. If only everything else in my life could be put on hold until I finish the book. That is not to be. I form new habits. I wake up at five-thirty and grab myself a hot coffee from the coffee maker that I programmed to have ready fifteen minutes before I rise.

I like this ritual of having coffee in bed, the room dark, Janet sleeping beside me. You'd laugh to see me with my 'bedhead' and a headlamp strapped across my upper forehead. I especially don't want to stumble into the newly placed IKEA shelving on my side of the room and wake Janet up while going for my 'black plasma.' The headlamp is set with a red filter that helps me see better in the dark and is not bright enough to disturb my wife' sleep. The red light reminds me of all the years I have spent in darkrooms.

Once a few sips have woken me up, (like rope-starting,) I pull out the IPAD Mini and its keyboard and begin typing. Usually I like what I write in the early morning. I began this habit of writing first thing in the day when I worked at CITY TV, in the old Hudson's Bay Building downtown. I'd get to work an hour before anyone else and sit at my desk and write my blog.

My old boss, Gord Sheppard, heard of my aspirations to write and he gave me valuable advice that has stuck with me since. He tells me, "if you want to be a writer, then you need to write every day. The best way to write every day is to have a blog." I see Gord himself has published a book after leaving CITY TV.

Being a bicycle commuter, it was easy to write about cycling and my involvement with Edmonton's cycling community gave me an audience. How pleased I was when people started to follow me and leave comments. I felt like a newspaper columnist who had readers expecting a frequent instalment. Being the literal person that I am, I called it "Bikewriter'sblog" and wrote it for nearly ten years. I really got into it. My photographic background helped make my blogs more interesting and a lot of the time I wanted them to be funny. Judging from the comments, I succeeded.

That early morning time of having the whole second floor of the Bay Building to myself was one of my favorite memories of the fifteen years I spent at the station. After parking my bike, I walked over to Slim Hortons and would order a medium black coffee, something I enjoyed sipping on for the whole hour. I had a comfortable chair, a great desk and a company computer. My camera was my work phone. I had everything I needed. Even my little notebooks, which I had been in the habit of filling with every day trivia, ever since the A-Channel strike, were full of jottings for future blogs.

The act of writing is not a new thing for me. I have written almost every day in my dream diaries since I was a teenager. I wanted somehow to prove that deja vu was simply something a person had dreamed. My thinking was that if I recorded my dreams, then perhaps I could prove my theory. I have hundreds and hundreds of dreams written in dozens of dream diaries. They are all written by hand

and usually with a fountain pen. I have yet to prove my theory.

I like using a fountain pen when writing by hand. I read somewhere that when you are learning something, the more senses you engage, the more likely you are to remember. My co-workers will often remark at my using a fountain pen to write. And it is not just any fountain pen. This is a fine writing instrument. A modern fountain pen that does not leak no matter what I am doing and how I am carrying it. I've taken it backpacking, bikepacking, mountain snow shoeing, everywhere and it has yet to fail me. Admittedly, the store where I bought it wasn't giving them away.

At an Edmonton Litfest book event a few years ago, author Ted Bishop was promoting his book "The Social Life of Ink" and he gave a presentation that involved everyone in the audience helping him make ink. He put a couple of Gaul nuts into a mortar with a pestle resting inside. Each audience member was instructed to give the pestle ten turns and with an audience of two hundred people, those Gaul nuts were turned into powder. When the mortar and pestle returned to the stage, Mr. Bishop added some liquid ingredients and voila! Ink!

While standing in line waiting to have him sign my copy of his book, I noticed he was using a fountain pen. He had taken the ink we had all helped make and was using it to sign his books. Ingenious: an author using audience-made ink to sign his book about ink.

When it was my turn, I marveled at his pen and when he let me handle it, I liked the feel of it between my fingers. He told me he had purchased it at STYLUS, a pen (read fine writing instrument) shop downtown. I happened to know the place from bike commuting past it twice a day. The next day I bought one and have enjoyed its use ever since.

My friend Keith gave me a different type of fountain pen for my birthday a few years ago. Keith collects a lot of things like Coleman lanterns (fifteen at last count,) bikes (he has twenty-two,) and sewing machines (ten, and he is the sewing machine whisperer.) He tells me he has hundreds of fountain pens but the one he gave me, he customized by carefully grinding the nib to match my right-handed writing style. It works so smoothly on paper that there is no concern about tearing it like I have done in the past, with less finely tuned fountain pens. I use the one Keith gave me to write in my diary, something I do every morning while I sip coffee and after recording my dream from the night before.

While writing this book, I attend a Litfest workshop on "How Much Truth is Too Much Truth?" given by author Angie Abdou. I find the subject to be intriguing. Janet, who is editing the book, has a strong reaction to something I have written about one of her family members. It was how I described this person. In my mind, the description is true. In her mind, it denigrates one of her family members. On my side of the family, I wrote about an event that took place on the night my father died. My sisters objected to a family member being shown in that light. I edited both stories out. Her family is like "My Big Fat Greek Wedding" and I am treading lightly.

In my notes from the workshop, Angie Abdou asks us to determine the price to be paid for writing about the truth. She has paid a price for some of her controversial writings. We are to ask ourselves the motivation for writing the truth. If it is for revenge, don't do it. That is not my motivation at all.

However, to keep the peace, I delete the passages about both families.

I was the last person to have Ms. Abdou sign her book and as she wrote, she asked me what I was writing. When I told her the premise of the "47-Year-Old-Present," she remembered the story. Before I leave the building, I see published author, Ruby Swanson, standing in the lobby. I tell her how much I enjoyed her humorous anecdote about one of her neighbours. When I tell her my name and what story I'm writing, she tells me she heard my interview on CBC radio and wishes me good luck with my project.

The workshop is full of authors, most of them published, and I come away a little bit worried. As I walk to my car, I think about some of these people reading my book and what they will think of it. Amateurish? Poorly written? Possibly.

I stop to pull out my fountain pen and write in my notebook: "These other writers might have a story and know how to write it, but in my case, I have a buzz going already."

I smile as I think to myself of someone reading my book and enjoying the story. My goal is to bring a little bit of sunshine to that person's life and I hope, Dear Reader, that I have succeeded.

ABOUT THE AUTHOR

 Adrian "Mike" Pearce, had a successful full time career as a television cameraman shooting for Canada's largest television networks.

Being an avid cyclist, he volunteers as a bicycle mechanic at BikeWorks North, a nonprofit community bike shop. He has been an ambassador for the Adventure Cycling Association and organizes bicycle camping trips every summer and fall for them.

This is Adrian Mike Pearce's first book.

32624450R00124

Made in the USA
Columbia, SC
08 November 2018